DATE DUE

Wagner

THE GREAT COMPOSERS

WAGNER

by

ELAINE PADMORE

THOMAS Y. CROWELL COMPANY

New York

7333950

First published in the United States of America in 1973

Copyright © 1971 by Elaine Padmore

Printed in Great Britain

Library of Congress Catalog Card No. 73–158698

ISBN 0–690–86511–2
0–690–86512–0 (LB)

Contents

Illustrations

LINE ILLUSTRATIONS

Illustrations

Music Examples

(all by Wagner)

I

The Boy

On the 22nd May 1813, in the German town of Leipzig, Johanna and Friedrich Wagner celebrated the arrival of their ninth baby, a boy. They christened him Wilhelm Richard. Sad to relate, father and son had only a brief acquaintance as Friedrich died five months later. Tired by overwork in his responsible post as a police official he had caught typhoid in an epidemic.

Apart from his large family, his greatest love had been the theatre, and his best friend, Ludwig Geyer, was an actor. This friend now proved a tower of strength to the bereaved family, and a year after Friedrich's death Ludwig married Johanna and took upon himself the care and education of her children.

Soon afterwards, he was offered an excellent job at the Royal Court Theatre in Dresden. In this town the family took up residence, and here Richard—the Wilhelm was soon dropped—grew to boyhood, surrounded by the magical sights and sounds of the theatre. He loved to watch his talented step-father act, and was fascinated too by the labyrinth of rooms that lay back-stage. There he discovered strange and often frightening treasure in the shape of exotic costumes, scenery and properties. The theatre was no place of entertainment to him, but a mysterious, fantastic world filled with shadowy spirits. He was irresistibly attracted to it, even though it gave him regular ghostly nightmares from which he awoke screaming, much to the annoyance of his brothers and sisters.

There was much for Richard to admire in his step-father, since Ludwig was a singer, writer and skilful portrait painter as well as a respected actor; but he too was soon to die and leave the family destitute once more. At the age of seven, Richard was sent to a little country school at Possendorf, not far from Dresden, to be taught by a clergyman. He had scarcely been there a year when the news came from Dresden that his step-father was gravely ill with a lung disease. At once Richard was taken home. His distracted mother asked him to pick out a tune on the piano, hoping to divert Ludwig's thoughts. The dying man listened in silence, then said to his wife, 'Is it possible he has musical talent?' The next morning he died.

One of his brothers now came to Johanna's aid. He had already given one of her older sons, Julius, an apprenticeship (he was a goldsmith), and now he offered to take care of the youngest, Richard, and see to his schooling in his own town of Eisleben. This arrangement lasted no more than a year as the guardian uncle then found himself a wife, and there was no longer room in his home for Richard. So back to Dresden he was sent. Here he found Johanna thriftily managing the household affairs and letting rooms to make money. Several of the older children were able to help as they now had jobs, mostly in the theatre. Albert, the eldest, and his second sister, Luisa, were at the theatre in Breslau, while Rosalie, the oldest girl, was at the Royal Court in Dresden, where Ludwig had acted. Another sister, Clara, was set on an operatic career and was having her lovely voice trained in preparation.

Johanna viewed her stage-struck family with some dismay and decided that at no cost should Richard tread the same risky path. Ludwig had 'hoped to make something of him', and Johanna felt it her duty to see that the dead man's fond wish was fulfilled. She had abandoned her own education at the age of fourteen in order to marry Friedrich Wagner: now she made up her mind that Richard should enjoy all the schooling she had missed and have his academic ability developed to the full. Unfortunately Richard was a rather reluctant scholar and his career at the Kreuz Grammar School in Dresden, to which he was now sent, was hardly such as to raise a mother's hopes. The only subject that really fired his imagination was Greek literature. He hated the grammar, and would learn no more of it than was strictly necessary for understanding the stories of the great mythological heroes, stories which he translated with loving care while he should have been concentrating on other lessons. He also wrote some original poetry in the classical manner. When the headmaster asked members of the school to submit poems commemorating the death of one of the boys, Richard's was singled out and published, much to the delight of his mother who had no doubt that her son would become a poet.

She had no reason to suspect he would be anything else for there was no sign at all of his musical genius. His brother Albert and sisters Rosalie and Clara were the musicians of the family. The house was full of music and musical talk, and often there were distinguished visitors like the composer Weber. Richard developed a passion for his opera *Der Freischütz* (*The*

Marksman), partly for its demonic supernatural story, but also for its thrilling music which he would beg his sisters to play for him. He tried to play bits of it himself, but only by ear as he had had no proper piano lessons. When he was twelve his mother agreed to let him learn, but he had no more desire to perfect his technique than he had to learn Greek grammar, and as soon as he could stumble through the overture to *Der Freischütz* he felt he had achieved his pianistic goal. As he came to like more pieces he wanted to copy them out and persuaded his mother to buy him manuscript paper, though she was far from happy with this development.

The band concerts in Dresden's parks gave him spine-chilling pleasures similar to those he had experienced earlier in the theatre. The very sound of the instruments tuning up was sufficient to put him in a state of fevered excitement. The violins tuning their fifths made him think of ghosts and spirits, while the A that the oboe sounds to give the orchestra the right pitch seemed to him like a call from the dead to rouse the other instruments.

In 1826 the family decided to move. Rosalie had accepted a good offer from a Prague theatre, and the family was to go there with her—all except Richard who had to stay behind at school. With no mother at hand to encourage his work, Richard found school more tiresome than ever. After lodging with a school friend's family for a time, he moved into a garret where he lived on coffee, wrote romantic verses and drafted the outline of a great Shakespearean tragedy. His summer visit to Leipzig in 1827 was a welcome change. The unfettered life of the university students in the town dazzled him. Their fancy clothes, gay customs and rude contempt for everyday conventions seemed to him utterly desirable: he would not be content until he was one of them.

School-days in Dresden became quite unbearable after this vision of freedom: he simply *had* to escape. Then one day sister Luisa came to visit him with the news that she was leaving the Breslau theatre and taking up a new post—in Leipzig. What was more, their mother and sisters had agreed to join her there. It was too much for Richard. He told his schoolmasters a made-up story of a sudden family summons and packed his things. His mother, alarmed to think of him pining away in a garret, gave her consent, and Richard left for Leipzig.

II

The Student

Leipzig was not the haven he had expected. The teachers at his new school, St. Nicholas's, saw fit to put him in a lower form than he had been in at Dresden, an indignity all the more painful since it meant giving up Homer in favour of the simpler Greek writers. Richard found a sympathetic friend in his Uncle Adolph Wagner, a very learned scholar who shared his nephew's contempt for the dull work he was set in school. Uncle Adolph's store of knowledge was much more to Richard's taste, for he was an expert on the Greek tragedies and other things besides. They went for long walks together each day and discussed great matters of philosophy and literature. Richard was often out of his depth but still clung eagerly to every word, as the mysteries of Dante, Goethe and Shakespeare were expounded to him.

Under this stimulus he secretly resumed work on the drama he had planned in Dresden. The result, freely based on many a famous tragedy, was a most gory tale of vengeance. The hero, like Hamlet, was visited by his slain father and told to avenge his wrongs; unlike Hamlet, this son had no time for thought but rapidly accomplished no less than forty-two murders in obedience to his father's wishes. Having disposed of so many characters in this way, Richard was obliged to bring them all back as ghosts at the end to witness the hero's demented death. He sent the finished manuscript to Uncle Adolph together with a letter asking him to explain to his mother and sisters that school was only hindering his free development. Uncle Adolph was filled with remorse for giving him such ideas, while the family regarded his great tragedy as a plain waste of time.

Richard was unperturbed, for he suddenly knew that no one could appreciate the true worth of his drama until he had set it to music. At the age of fifteen he had glimpsed his vocation for the first time. Since his arrival in Leipzig he had developed a passion for Beethoven: now he wanted to write similar heroic music for his tragedy. To discover the neces-

Above, left: Wagner's
mother, Johanna and
above, right, his step-
father, Ludwig Geyer;
below, The Red and
White Lion, Leipzig,
where Richard Wag-
ner was born in 1813.
The inn was demol-
ished in 1886

Wagner in Paris, 1842, a
pencil drawing by his
friend Ernst Benedikt
Kietz

The composer's first wife, Minna
Planer, whom he married in
1839

sary techniques he borrowed a musical textbook from the library and secretly had harmony lessons from a violinist in the Leipzig orchestra. All too soon he was discontented. 'For me,' he wrote later, 'music was a spirit, a noble and mystic monster, and any attempt to regulate it seemed to lower it in my eyes.' Learning about the keys and chords of music was no more to his liking than declining the verbs and nouns of Greek literature: both served only as means to an end, and as soon as he had the barest grasp of harmony and counterpoint, Richard began to compose.

First there was a piano sonata in D minor, then a string quartet (as soon as he had mastered the alto clef for the viola), an orchestral aria for soprano, and the beginnings of a pastoral play for which he made up the words at the same instant as the music. He was so engrossed he forgot all about school, until the summer of 1829 when Johanna was informed that her son had not attended for the last six months. When her anger subsided she sadly faced the fact that, in spite of all her hopes to the contrary, Richard was going to be a musician. She decided to make the best of it, and in return for his promise to go back to school, agreed to pay for his harmony and violin lessons. More important to him than these were the lessons he learned from copying out the symphonies of his beloved Beethoven. The Ninth Symphony, then considered all that was fantastic and incomprehensible in music, had a special hold upon him. He studied it for hours, and even made a piano version of it, which he sent off to the publisher Schott, who thanked him for his pains with a score of the *Missa Solemnis in D*.

He was quite overwhelmed by Beethoven's opera *Fidelio* which he saw starring the greatest singer of the day, Wilhelmine Schröder-Devrient. When it was over he sent a note telling her that from that moment his life 'had acquired its true significance, and that if in the days to come she should ever hear my name praised in the world of Art, she must remember that she had that evening made me what I then swore it was my destiny to become'. He longed to compose operas, great works that would be worthy of so wonderful a singer; but as yet it was beyond his power. For a time he drowned his frustrated ambitions in the gay life of Leipzig. His school work went from bad to worse. By Easter 1830 it was quite clear that no member of the staff at St. Nicholas's would ever dream of recommending Wagner to the university. Since that was still his ambition it was decided that he should leave school, study privately for six months and then go to the rival St. Thomas's school to qualify for the university. But revolution was in the air that summer, and Wagner's thoughts were far from his studies. The first uprising was in Paris in July when the French overthrew

Charles X, their tyrant king, for a more enlightened ruler. The urge for freedom spread swiftly over Europe, and Leipzig had its share of upheavals. Wagner was full of political ideas and enthusiastically joined in the student demonstrations, but when real violence broke out in the town the students came over to the side of law and order and helped the authorities to keep the peace. They were made home guards and patrolled the town, protecting threatened citizens and their property. When they were off duty, Wagner and his friends drank, gambled and argued about politics. School started again and St. Thomas's proved every bit as loathsome as its predecessor. Once again he began composing, this time an orchestral *Overture in B flat*, very reminiscent of Beethoven. Much to his delight, Heinrich Dorn, the young conductor at the Leipzig theatre promised to perform it at a concert for the poor on Christmas Eve.

It was rather a mystical work, with the three main sections of the orchestra having quite distinct characters: the music of the brass was 'black', that of the strings 'red' and the wind themes 'green'. Wagner even intended to write out the score in these colours if only he could have found some green ink. The performance was a total disaster. He had quite miscalculated the effect of having a loud drum beat after every fourth bar. 'What the listeners must have thought when "black", "red" and "green" themes became intermingled, has always remained a mystery to me,' he wrote, 'for the fatal drum-beat, brutally hammered out, entirely deprived me of my senses, especially as this prolonged and continually recurring effect now began to rouse, not only the attention but the merriment of the audience. I heard my neighbours calculating the return of this effect; knowing the absolute correctness of their calculations, I suffered a thousand torments.' At last the awful nightmare was over. It was a sufficiently gruelling experience to make him abandon the other musical projects he was toying with at the time and throw himself with renewed vigour into the excesses of student life.

In February 1831 he at last joined his friends at the university when he enrolled as a music student. He spent the first few dizzy months gambling away every penny he could find—including his mother's pension, which mercifully he won back with his last coin. His quick tongue and argumentative nature caused him to be challenged to duels on several occasions, but though he was always ready to fight, his opponents mysteriously failed to appear. For his mother's sake he at last returned to serious study. Since entering the university he had been learning harmony and counterpoint with Theodor Weinlig who had the post once held by Bach—that of choirmaster and organist at St. Thomas's Church. This worthy man had placed Wagner on a strict course of four-part harmony exercises to which he responded with sparing enthusiasm. Weinlig was on the point of dropping his unrewarding pupil, but now Wagner promised to try his hardest and within eight weeks had so mastered the intricacies of fugue and counterpoint that his surprised teacher declared that he could teach him nothing more.

⊦ He was now allowed to compose what he pleased and quickly produced three overtures, a *Symphony in C major* and some piano music, including the *Polonaise in D* for four hands. All were built on the sound principles of Beethoven and Mozart whose techniques he had carefully studied. This time when the works were performed in public, there was no nightmare for Wagner and no dissatisfaction from the listeners.

The joys of university life soon palled and within a year he was sickened by the selfishness and over-indulgence of his student existence. In the summer of 1832 he left the university for good. For a while he shook the dust of Leipzig from his feet and went on a long holiday to Vienna and Prague. In Vienna he visited the opera; in Prague he began one of his own, a gruesome work called *The Wedding* in which the bride pushes an unwanted lover over a high parapet and reveals her guilt when she dies, insane, at his funeral. The whole of the libretto was completed and the dark-toned music well under way when Wagner returned home in the late autumn. At once he offered the new work for the approval of his favourite sister Rosalie, but she immediately declared it too relentlessly gloomy to succeed on the stage. Without bitterness Wagner bowed to her opinion and consigned his manuscript to the waste-bin.

Compensation came that winter when his *Symphony* was performed in a Leipzig concert and most favourably received by the music critics. He was soon busily planning another opera, this time a magical work called *Die Feen* (*The Fairies*). With this libretto in his bag he set out from Leipzig in January 1833, his destination the town of Würzburg, where his first job awaited him.

Polonaise in D for piano duet

Allegro maestoso

III

The Apprentice

At that time, Wagner's brother Albert was working at the Würzburg theatre in the dual capacity of tenor and stage manager. When the post of chorus-master fell vacant he thought at once of Richard, almost twenty years old, unemployed, and wholly dependent on his mother. It was quite a humble job and poorly paid, but it taught Wagner much about the realities of life in a small German opera-house. Like most others of its kind, the Würzburg company had cheerfully low standards of performance, and intrepidly regaled its audiences with an ambitious range of fashionable operas. In the process of teaching the chorus their parts Wagner got to know the repertoire thoroughly. He witnessed the popular success of romantic fantasy operas like Weber's *Freischütz* and Marschner's *Vampire*, and on such models based his own *Fairies*.

When the season finished he went home to his mother and Rosalie and proudly played and sang his way through the completed opera. They were most impressed, and Rosalie wasted no time in persuading the director of the Leipzig theatre to stage the work. But time passed, excuse followed excuse, and no production materialized. As hope faded, so did Wagner's liking for romantic opera. In an anonymous article he denounced Weber and his 'solid' German music, and praised instead the vibrant, sensuous melodies of Bellini and Rossini.

Schröder-Devrient was largely responsible for his abrupt change of heart. In the spring of 1834 she enthralled Wagner by her thrilling performance in a Bellini opera and made him conscious of the real human passions surging through the music. German opera suddenly struck his ears as being too dry and earnest, and much too lost in thought to have real red blood in its veins. Like other 'advanced' young men of his time he was infatuated with the passionate Italian south and tired of the cold morality of Germany. Sober, pensive music was not for the exuberant young man who had recently discovered his attractiveness to the young ladies of the Würzburg chorus! Before long he was planning an Italian opera that matched his mood exactly. Its name was *Das Liebesverbot* (*The Love Ban*), and though it started out as a version of Shakespeare's *Measure for Measure*, Wagner had soon transformed the plot so it exalted sensuality and decried stuffy puritanism.

Not surprisingly, he accepted his next job for the sake of a pretty woman. The director of the Leipzig theatre much regretted his hasty promise to stage *The Fairies*. A useful way out of his embarrassment was to recommend Wagner for an out-of-town post, that of musical director of the Magdeburg theatrical troupe. Wagner disliked being staved off, but all the same decided to inspect the company. He found them giving a summer season of operas and plays at the tiny spa town of Lauchstädt, and a more decrepit little group he could scarcely have hoped to meet. The manager, Heinrich Bethmann, greeted him in dressing-gown and nightcap and gave him a detailed account of his internal complaints. His lame wife reclined on a couch, with an admirer, the company's elderly bass, devotedly seated at her side. Schmale, the stage manager, greedily reached for fruit from a cherry tree outside the window and loudly ejected the stones from his toothless gums as he conversed with Wagner. After politely informing them that he would certainly *not* be joining their company, Wagner made his escape and went out into the town to find somewhere to spend the night. An actor escorted him to a suitable boarding-house, and there at the door was Minna Planer. She was the troupe's leading actress, a girl some three-and-a-half years older than Wagner. He saw her fresh beauty and immaculate appearance and was captivated. If only he had returned to Leipzig without seeing her he would have spared them both thirty years' unhappiness; as it was he reversed his decision about the job, booked a room near hers, rushed off home to collect his luggage and was back in time to conduct *Don Giovanni* the next Sunday.

It was the first opera he had ever conducted and a lesser man would have quailed at so sudden an introduction to the art, but Wagner's supreme self-confidence carried him through. Before long he had established quite a local reputation for himself as a conductor. Bethmann's troupe proved every bit as disreputable as Wagner had first suspected: it was badly run, and so impoverished that wages were often weeks overdue. The repertoire Wagner had to conduct consisted mostly of worthless light operas, but he accepted his lot cheerfully for the sake of Minna Planer. Because she was no easy conquest his determination to win her was all the stronger. He flung caution to the winds and pursued her ruthlessly, careless of the gaping void that separated their personalities. A sympathetic nature and considerable domestic skill were Minna's chief assets: of imagination and intellect she had but little. True, she was unlike the other flighty actresses, but her values were very different from his. She regarded her theatrical talent as a built-in means to a good living, and aspired to an ultimate goal of financial security and middle-class respectability. Polite aloofness greeted the many wooers who could not further her ambition: Wagner was one of them until he wore her down with his overwhelming charm and confident promises of coming fame. In fact he cared little for the conventional aims cherished by Minna. He was wild, reckless and extravagant, always in debt, always borrowing, rarely repaying; but he was also iron-willed and, having set his heart on Minna, was not to be thwarted.

Autumn came and the company returned to its Magdeburg home. When he was not busy conducting, he composed. He produced a rousing *Neujahrs-Kantate* (*New Year Cantata*) for performance on the first day of 1835 and an overture to a play called *Columbus* which the company staged in February. The real highlight of the season for Wagner was when Schröder-Devrient herself made a few guest appearances under his baton. She was so taken with the brilliant young conductor that she promised to come back and sing in his charity concert at the end of the season. This concert should easily have paid off his accumulated debts, but, unfortunately, it was sabotaged by his own extravagance and the distrust of the Magdeburgers. The wary citizens could not believe that so great a singer would return to their little town so soon, and refused to be hoodwinked into buying tickets. Unsuspecting, Wagner rashly engaged a large and expensive orchestra for the event and confidently invited his debtors to present their claims outside his hotel room the morning after. It was one of the rare occasions in Schröder-Devrient's career when she sang to a near-empty house, and one of the frequent occasions in Wagner's when furious debtors had to be appeased by glib talk and fervent promises.

The opera season ended and Wagner's appointment with it. There was nothing for it but to retreat to Leipzig and throw himself once more on the kind hearts and open purses of his family. Minna stayed behind as the dramatic season was not yet over. The separation proved an agony, and Wagner made up his mind to return to her at Magdeburg next season whether he got paid or not. As it happened, the King of Prussia came to the rescue of Bethmann's bankrupt company and Wagner was offered a better salary than before. He gaily set off on a summer tour of Germany to discover new and better singers for Magdeburg. When he returned he enlarged the orchestra too, and persuaded the singers and bandsmen of a nearby army unit to swell the ranks on occasion, in return for free tickets.

His pleasure in the much improved standards was abruptly shattered in November when Minna left the company. The new season had brought with it a rival leading actress, Madame Grabowsky, wife of the chief stage manager. The roles that were rightfully Minna's were suddenly assigned to this usurper. With no thought for Wagner the offended Minna accepted an offer from Berlin's Königstadt Theatre, and departed. Wagner was beside himself. He besieged her with fierce imploring letters. He battled with the management over her rights. In desperation he proposed to her—and she accepted. She came back, and he quickly finished *The Love Ban* and pinned to it their joint hopes for a great financial success on which to marry.

It was to be produced at the very end of the season, March 1836, as a benefit for Wagner. Bethmann cunningly arranged that proceeds from the first performance should go to cover management costs, and those from the second should line Wagner's pockets. Alas, there was no second performance. The first was a complete fiasco. It took place after only ten days of rehearsals during which Wagner vigorously assisted the singers by continuous prompting. Without his shouted aid they were at a loss to remember their parts, and the performance itself was so much mouthing, la-la-ing, and filling-in from other operas. No audience gathered for the second night, so it mattered little that fifteen minutes before curtain-up the prima donna's husband punched the second tenor on the nose, and started such a brawl among the company that any performance that night was out of the question.

So the season ended. Wagner's many creditors lost patience with him and tried to have him arrested, but he evaded them by lying low for a few weeks. His next move was to Berlin where his hopes of getting *The Love Ban* produced came to nothing. Minna met with more success. She found herself a new post at Königsberg and Wagner soon joined her there. The conductor's post was already filled, but as the holder, a man called Schuberth, intended to leave quite soon, Minna persuaded the management to promise Wagner the job and to pay him a small retaining fee until it fell vacant.

Months passed and Schuberth still hung on, causing Wagner untold misery and humiliation. To the company he was an outsider, merely Minna's fiancé. To Schuberth he was a dangerous rival to be treated with suspicion and hostility. In spite of all, he managed to compose a '*Rule, Britannia*' Overture which he conducted at a winter concert. He hated the dull town, the cold weather, his poverty and the men who flattered Minna. They bickered often, but his jealousy spurred him on to marry her. 'Her agreeable and soothing qualities still had such a beneficial effect on me,' he wrote, 'that with the frivolity natural to me, as well as the obstinacy with which I met all opposition, I silenced the inner voice that darkly foreboded disaster.' The wedding took place on 24th November 1836. Wagner was twenty-three years old.

Disaster struck the very next day when he was summoned before the magistrate to answer the charges of his Magdeburg creditors. By this time he was even deeper in debt, for the luxurious furniture that adorned their new flat was obtained entirely on credit. In April 1837 he was appointed conductor in succession to Schuberth, just in time to save the household goods from being reclaimed. One month later the theatre went bankrupt. It was more than Minna could bear. She packed her bags and fled with a wealthy merchant named Dietrich. Heartbroken and outraged by turns, Wagner pursued her to her parents' house in Dresden. He gave her news of a well-paid conductorship offered him at Riga, and by tinting his future prospects with a rosy hue, induced her to come back to him. They spent a few relatively peaceful weeks in the country near Dresden, but then she deserted him again.

Fortunately his sister Ottilie and her husband were at hand to give consolation. They were the sort of refined and sensitive people he most needed just then to raise him from his demoralized state and restore his creative impulse. At their home he laid plans to turn Bulwer Lytton's historical novel, *Rienzi*, into an opera. When he went to Riga in September he began to turn the plans into reality. *Rienzi* became his escape from the uncongenial life of the theatre. He had been given the job because of his professed admiration for sensuous Italianate opera: now disillusioned in love and sobered in taste he was out of sympathy with such works, which were, unfortunately, the staple fare of the Riga theatre. His taste for more serious art and his zealous attempts to raise the company's standards made him unpopular among the lax, easy-going theatre folk. Increasingly he identified himself with the hero of his new opera, for Rienzi, last of the Roman tribunes, was the one man with ideals and nobility among the thousands of a dissolute society. The mean denizens of Germany's provincial theatres were deaf to the prophet in their midst: therefore the prophet would have to seek recognition in a foreign land.

Another German, Meyerbeer, had captivated Paris with his grand operas, epic works in which Italian, French and German features were cleverly fused into an international whole. Vital ingredients of such operas were

The Apprentice

military spectacles, conflagrations, massacres, scenic wonders, lavish ballets, huge choruses, high sentiments and pompous music. Accordingly Wagner decked out *Rienzi* with similar embellishments and began to put out feelers towards Paris.

Rienzi: from the overture

A contrite Minna returned to him a few weeks after his arrival in Riga and did her best to make life there more tolerable for him. Then unexpectedly, in the spring of 1839, Wagner lost his job. He believed a managerial conspiracy had ousted him, but the official reason, a highly plausible one, was his alarming financial situation which might occasion a hasty exit from the town at any moment. Whatever the cause, the effect was decisive enough: his scheme to leave Germany was put into action. In June 1839, with no reputation to speak of, an incomplete grand opera and scarcely a word of French, Wagner set out to conquer Paris.

IV

The Paris Venture

The journey was full of perils and mishaps. There were no railways in Germany in those days so the choice lay between stage-coach or a sea voyage. Wagner chose the latter, partly because it was cheaper but also because it was the only way to take their enormous Newfoundland dog, Robber. As a debtor liable to flee, Wagner's passport had been taken from him by the authorities, so the three of them had to be smuggled over the Russian border, which lay between them and their port of embarkation. This dangerous escapade was organized by faithful friends and took place under cover of night. There were just a few minutes at the changing of the watch when formalities diverted the guards' eyes from the frontier: that was the moment when Wagner, Minna and the dog had to tear down the hill, scramble across a ditch and run on until they were beyond the range of the soldiers' guns. 'I was simply at a loss to convey to my poor exhausted wife how extremely I regretted the whole affair,' wrote Wagner later.

This was not the last of their troubles, for a fearful sea voyage followed. The small ship *Thetis*, with a crew of seven, was to carry them to London, and then they would sail to France by steamer. The voyage usually took eight days: this time it lasted three-and-a-half weeks. After being becalmed for a week, a violent storm drove them miles off course to Norway, where they took shelter in a fjord. Impatiently the captain put to sea again too soon and the vessel was tossed upon a reef. The damage she sustained was much less than the terror and shock suffered by those aboard her. After a few repairs they set forth once more and were soon in the midst of a severe hurricane. Wagner and Minna were terribly sick and afraid. As the ship heaved at the mercy of the wild waves, and lightning ripped open the skies they thought their last hour had come. Eventually the storm abated and the coast of England loomed ahead, though even when approaching the Thames the ship was in constant danger of being flung on to sandbanks by the fierce westerly gale.

Ill and exhausted, Wagner and Minna finally disembarked and cheered themselves up with a week's sightseeing. Wagner visited the House of Lords in hopes of encountering Lord Lytton, the author of *Rienzi*, but he was out of town. He was allowed to hear a debate, and was thrilled to see the great Duke of Wellington and Lord Melbourne, the Prime Minister, among those discussing the anti-slavery bill. On 20th August he left London and sailed with wife and dog across the Channel to Boulogne 'where we took leave of the sea with a fervent desire never to go on it again'.

It happened that Meyerbeer was spending the summer at that same port, so Wagner was able to meet him straightaway. The great man treated him most kindly and had him call again several times. He enthused over *Rienzi* and wrote glowing letters recommending Wagner to important Parisian musicians. In high spirits Wagner descended on the French capital. One by one he visited the recipients of Meyerbeer's letters, and little by little his spirits sank. The manager of the Paris Opéra did not want to know him. Habeneck the conductor could offer no more than to run through his *Columbus* Overture at a Conservatoire rehearsal. The singers he plied with songs of various sorts liked them well enough, but could not promise to perform them.

Wagner would have been at a loss were it not for the new friends who quickly gathered around him. His sisters Luisa and Cecilia were in Paris with their husbands and were able to introduce Wagner to some members of the German colony: Anders, a music librarian, his house-mate Lehrs, a translator, and Kietz, a kind-hearted painter who worked so laboriously that 'he complained because some of his sitters died before their portraits were completed'. They all racked their brains for imaginative schemes to launch Wagner into Parisian musical life, but to no avail. His funds soon ran out and he had to visit the pawnbroker with Minna's expensive theatrical costumes and their wedding presents. At last Meyerbeer arrived in Paris and gave him more introductions, to his agent Gouin, and to Schlesinger, a publisher who could offer him some journalism and hack-work. Months of distressing poverty went by before Gouin shed a ray of hope: at Easter 1840 he announced that *The Love Ban* was to be produced at the Théâtre de la Renaissance.

Wagner was wildly excited by this reversal of fortune and moved into a more expensive flat and furnished it nicely. No sooner was this done than news came that the theatre had gone bankrupt. His disappointment and remorse were terrible, and so too was his shame that he had resorted to *The Love Ban*, 'that superficial early work'. 'Of course I had only done this because

I thought I should win success more rapidly in Paris by adapting myself to its frivolous taste. My aversion from this kind of taste, which had long been growing, coincided with my abandonment of all hopes of success in Paris.'

An important cause of this aversion was his rekindled passion for Beethoven. He heard the excellent Conservatoire orchestra playing the Ninth Symphony more wonderfully than he had dreamed possible. Having endured disappointment and misfortune Wagner thought that he now understood the suffering he heard in Beethoven's noble music. He wanted to make his own works express the same emotions. The first result, even before *The Love Ban* disaster, was a tragic overture to *Faust*. Now in the spring of 1840 he planned to express these deep feelings in a new opera, *Der Fliegende Holländer* (*The Flying Dutchman*), based on a story that haunted him on that nightmare voyage to London. It was the ancient legend of a sailor who was condemned by the devil to rove the sea endlessly until freed by a woman's love. Wagner no longer felt like Rienzi the conquering hero but the lonely Dutchman, travelling a storm-tossed path in search of love and understanding. While the libretto took shape he resumed work on the last part of *Rienzi*: since it told of the hero's downfall it suited Wagner's mood.

None of this activity brought any money to the needy household and it was decided that lodgers might ease the situation. A miserly old lady from Leipzig was the first, succeeded by an agreeable German commercial traveller who played the flute in his spare time. Wagner earned a little money from articles written for Schlesinger, but was flabbergasted when asked to devise him a teaching manual for the cornet. He knew absolutely nothing about this instrument, except that it was the latest craze of Parisian amateurs, and was unable to oblige. Schlesinger replaced this request with a demand for fourteen suites of popular operatic airs arranged for this instrument; he sent Wagner no less than sixty opera scores to work from. It was a very dull task and Wagner was not sorry to be relieved of it half-way through when an expert cornet player inspected his efforts and declared most of of them unplayable.

It was good to get back to *Rienzi*, and by the end of November 'this most voluminous of all my operas' was complete. Wagner knew by now that it was useless to seek a Paris performance: if Germany would have his opera he could justifiably return and be rid of this Paris that snubbed him. It was to Dresden's Royal Court that he sent the score. This theatre of his childhood was now rebuilt and up to date. Schröder-Devrient was singing there, and so was the famous heroic tenor Tichatschek who would make an ideal Rienzi. The acceptance and success of this grandest of grand operas would mean so much, and at present Wagner had so little; he was even being threatened with imprisonment for debt. Fortunately Schlesinger saved him from imminent starvation by giving him an advance on another task, that of arranging Donizetti's opera *La Favorita* for a host of different instruments (including the cornet!). This monotonous labour lasted the winter. No sooner was it done than misfortune struck again. Wagner and Minna had meant to leave their expensive flat, but being ignorant of the Paris customs they gave notice to the landlord a day too late. It meant they would have to pay the rent for another whole year. Luckily they managed to let the flat for a few months, so were able to move to cheap quarters at Meudon, on the outskirts, a move that was 'no more than a flight from the impossible into the unknown', for how they were going to live during the following summer they 'had not the faintest idea'.

Journalism was the only solution, though it scarcely kept the wolf from the door. In July, penniless and hungry, Wagner was forced to suffer a severe blow to his pride for the sake of a few hundred francs. A year before, he had taken the plot of *The Flying Dutchman* to the manager of the Opéra and offered to set it as a one-act work. The manager kept the plot to look at, and now offered to buy it for 500 francs—for some other composer to set to music. Wagner was insulted but too poor to argue. As he accepted the money he vowed silently that it must last until he had worked out *The Flying Dutchman* as a great new three-act work for Germany. His resolution was helped by the longed-for news from Dresden: *Rienzi* was accepted.

The work he now sat down to write was going to be different from all other operas. He had seen the grand spectaculars of Meyerbeer and Spontini, the romances of Marschner and Weber and the gay comedies of Auber and Rossini. All of them, it seemed to him, erred in the same direction: they aimed to show off voices rather than present a drama in music. He wanted to remedy this by changing the formal structure that allowed it to happen. Instead of the usual chain of separate arias and choruses he would write one long expanse of music, like a Beethoven symphony. As in those symphonies, there would be themes that came back several times, interacting and developing. Since Wagner's music had characters to act out its drama, each of the themes could be associated with one of them. So this stark motive, hurled out by the brass at the opening of the stormy overture, belongs to the cursed Dutchman:

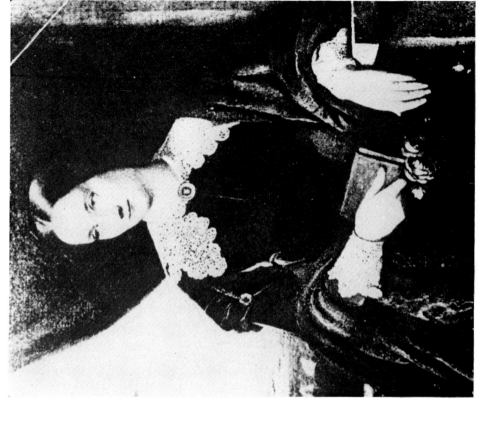

Mathilde Wesendonck, c. 1850

The warrant for Wagner's arrest made out in Dresden, 16th May 1849. It applied not only to Saxony but to all other German states

The earliest known photograph
of Richard Wagner taken in
Paris, *c.* 1848

Hans von Bülow, ardent admirer of
Wagner and first husband of Liszt's
daughter, Cosima

Cosima von Bülow, who later became
Wagner's wife

and this gentle one, first played on the *cor anglais* (English horn), to Senta's redeeming love:

It was two or three operas later before he learned to make a really continuous symphony of such recurring themes, but even so, there are fewer breaks in *The Flying Dutchman* than in any previous work in the history of opera.

Not all the sea music is as wild and storm-tossed as the Overture; the third act starts with a jovial, shanty-like 'Sailors' Song' where only occasional chromatic runs suggest the rising swell of the sea.

Sailors' Song from *The Flying Dutchman*

It took Wagner just seven weeks to finish this opera, which he called a 'music-drama'. As he completed the last scene, the 500 francs ran out. Summer was over and it was necessary to return to Paris, but they had no money and were forced to rely on the kindness of Kietz to pay the rent of their tiny new apartment. The flat which they had let for the summer was now empty and Wagner was obliged to give the landlord the furniture in lieu of rent. Kietz brought money, a few francs at a time, while Wagner sat at home orchestrating the new work and composing the overture. He could hardly have gone out in any case as his shoes were quite soleless. By the beginning of December the full score was ready and was soon on its way to the Berlin Opera.

Another dreary winter of opera-arranging passed, but nothing could damp Wagner's spirits now there was a hope of escape. His thoughts were full of Germany, which, since it had accepted one of his works now presented itself to his mind 'in a wholly new and ideal light'. He was in constant touch with Dresden, and at last the production date of *Rienzi* was settled. Now the wealthier side of his family began to take interest. Luisa gave him 500 francs, and when in February *The Flying Dutchman* was accepted in Berlin, her husband was sufficiently impressed to provide money for Wagner and Minna to return home. The long-awaited day arrived: on the 7th April 1842 they parted from the good friends who had shared their poverty and distress. With tears of sorrow mingled with hopes of joy, they left Paris for Dresden.

From the very first rehearsal *Rienzi* seemed destined for success. The singers loved the music and were anxious to please this fascinating composer who had suddenly emerged from total obscurity. Tichatschek liked one part so much that he thought it should be paid for at every sing-through; he took out a coin and the rest of the cast gaily followed suit. 'From that day forward, whenever we came to this passage at rehearsals, the cry was raised, "Here comes the silver-penny part", and Schröder-Devrient, as she took out her purse, remarked that these rehearsals would ruin her.' The proceeds from this piece of fun were regularly handed to Wagner. Little did the donors know that they were the vital providers of his daily food!

A caricature of Wagner by himself

Dresden was in an exceptional state of excitement at the prospect of the first night, so glowing were the reports spread abroad by the cast. That first night, 20th October 1842, was the turning point in Wagner's fortunes. *Rienzi* was a spectacular success and Wagner was cheered loud and long. He was famous overnight. The theatre management quickly decided that on no account should Berlin have the honour of presenting *The Flying Dutchman*; its first performance must be given in Dresden. This was duly arranged and the first night took place the following January. It was not such a triumph. The audience expected another *Rienzi* complete with battles, processions, ballets, dazzling costumes and all. The *Dutchman* seemed strange, gloomy and uneventful by comparison. Wagner was disappointed with the performance. The scenic effects were poorly done, and Wächter, who played the Dutchman, was very fat, wooden, and quite unable to convey the right emotion: in addition the orchestra was too small to give the rich, full tone Wagner wanted. He could see that still better equipped theatres and singers would be needed to present his new works properly.

Meanwhile, various important musical posts in Dresden were offered him. The one he accepted carried with it honour, prestige, and a life salary of 4,500 marks a year. It was the position of Court Conductor. He was so very highly regarded that the usual custom of serving a probationary year was waived in his case. Such was the measure of his achievement—and only months ago he had been starving and unwanted in Paris.

V

The Royal Conductor

Numerous misgivings clouded Wagner's mind as he took the oath of loyalty to the King. His past experiences of theatrical life warned him that even a court theatre was to be avoided, and especially one where an officious and rigid ruling body held sway. But the allurements of social position and handsome salary were irresistible after years of penury—and besides he wanted to please Minna.

The drawbacks of his decision soon became apparent. In no time his creditors swooped down, cherishing greater hopes of repayment from the royal conductor to the King of Saxony than from the impecunious musical director of various insignificant theatres. A large loan from Schröder-Devrient helped him to pay off the more threatening of them. He found, too, that holders of royal appointments were subject to envy and spite from their subordinates, as demonstrated by his dealings with the leader of the orchestra. Lipinsky was a first-class violinist but an arrogant leader: he always liked to come in a shade before the other violins so his playing could be heard individually. He did not take kindly to Wagner's attempts to break him of this habit, and tried his best to turn the whole orchestra against their new conductor. When an aged bass player died, Lipinsky suggested to Wagner that the vacancy be filled by a skilful player from outside, instead of by promotion within the ranks of the orchestra. The custom whereby a vacancy was invariably filled by the next most senior player, regardless of his competence, seemed absurd to Wagner and he was pleased to break it. When he announced his decision to the orchestra they turned on him as one man, and the treacherous Lipinsky accused him of trying to undermine their rights. Wagner took care to trust no court employee after that episode.

Socially he enjoyed his new position. He could number Schumann, Mendelssohn, Marschner and Hiller among his musical acquaintances, and found in Liszt a true and lifelong friend. The Dresden Choral Society invited him to become its conductor and as a result, in the summer of 1843, he found himself directing the massed male voice choirs of Saxony in a gala concert. Twelve hundred voices rang out in a performance of *Das Liebesmahl der Apostel* (*The Love Feast of the Apostles*), a dramatic cantata he had written for the occasion. This and similar events aimed to raise money for a special project. Weber had once served Dresden faithfully in the position that Wagner now held. His remains lay in London, in a remote corner of St. Paul's, and the Choral Society thought it proper that he should be solemnly brought home to Dresden and there laid to rest. Wagner gave his whole-hearted support because Weber's music was the first he had loved. The following year the plan came to fruition. Wagner arranged some of Weber's opera *Euryanthe* to accompany the funeral procession, and at the graveside delivered a moving oration. Some of the best singers from the opera then performed a solemn choral piece he had composed.

Most of his work centred around the opera-house, but he found that the court conductor was also expected to write 'occasional' music for state events. Just as Handel wrote music for the royal fireworks and the royal trip up the Thames, so Wagner wrote music for the unveiling of a royal statue and for the return of his monarch from a long stay in England. The idea for this 'welcome home' ode was all his own and was a gesture of pure affection for his royal employer. He rehearsed some three hundred choristers and a hundred-and-twenty bandsmen, and even got them to march through the castle grounds so that dreamily receding strains could be heard from the royal vantage point.

He acquired a comfortable home in Dresden and filled it with furnishings and costly books well beyond his means. In his library were works of old and medieval German literature, histories of the Middle Ages and books on the German people in general. He also bought the great works of world literature in their original languages, intending to learn them some day. During the first few months of his appointment he was often to be seen reading Grimm's *German Mythology*. He felt himself 'enchained by a wondrous magic' to the shadowy figures of the legendary world, 'a world revealed as it were by miracle'. He became convinced that myth and legend were the only subjects opera should deal with. In January 1844 he wrote about this to his friend Karl Gaillard. The playwright, he told him, may draw his subjects from the present time, but the opera composer must 'conjure up the holy spirit of poetry which has come down to us from the legends and sagas of past ages'. This way opera could raise itself from the 'debasement' into which it had fallen because composers treated 'commonplaces, intrigues, etc., subjects which spoken drama and comedy are far more succesful in presenting'. He went on, 'I have chosen for my next opera the beautiful and characteristic saga of the knight Tannhäuser, who dwelt in the Venusberg and then went to Rome on a pilgrimage to seek absolution.' This saga had first taken his fancy towards the end of his Paris days. Now, amid the distractions of his new life, he was busily turning it into an opera.

A little while before it was finished, Wagner enjoyed a pleasant diversion: Spontini, the grand opera composer, came to conduct his *La Vestale* at the theatre. Usually the standard of performance was fairly mediocre, and even Wagner was powerless to raise it when tied by red tape to outmoded procedures. Spontini as a venerated outsider had much more freedom. He shook the management considerably with his demand for 'twelve good double basses'. To Wagner's delight he insisted on regrouping the orchestra, an excellent change that would normally have cost the Court Conductor months of argument with officialdom.

In the summer of 1845 while the medieval costumes for *Tannhäuser* were being carefully stitched, and the scenery expensively painted by Europe's best designers, over at the Paris Opéra, Wagner went to Bohemia on holiday. It was a marvellous hot summer, and he spent the lazy days reading legends and taking the waters at Marienbad. *Lohengrin*, the legend of the swan, gripped his imagination. He wanted to turn it into a libretto at once, but the feverish excitement of creation was likely to undo the good done by the restful water-cure. Instead he fixed his thoughts on a lighter story, from the Middle Ages —Hans Sachs the cobbler and the Mastersingers of Nuremberg. Before long it took the shape of a comic opera in his mind, but it could not keep him from *Lohengrin*. One day at noon he climbed into the prescribed bath in which he was meant to soak for an hour. Suddenly the desire to write *Lohengrin* overwhelmed him: he jumped out of the bath, dressed in a great hurry and dashed home to start work. Within a few days he had sketched out the whole opera. The doctors at the spa quite despaired of him and told him he should give up taking the waters as he was a most unsuitable subject.

In September rehearsals of *Tannhäuser* began in earnest. Tichatschek was to sing the title role, Schröder-Devrient the seductive Venus, and Albert Wagner's daughter Johanna the young and saintly Elizabeth. Schröder-Devrient was soon in despair over her part. 'What on earth am I to wear as Venus?' she asked, only too conscious that at her age she could scarcely sport the flimsy and alluring garments most suited to the goddess of love. Tichatschek's problem was more crucial for, in Wagner's words, he was 'a singer incapable of dramatic seriousness, whose natural gifts only fitted him for joyous or declamatory accents, and who was totally incapable of expressing pain and suffering'. Wagner was at a loss to make his friend understand Tannhäuser's mental anguish, and in the end had to stop trying as it only made Tichatschek nervous and confused. The dilemma facing Tannhäuser was the basic choice between good and evil: no sooner has he fixed his mind on one than desire for the other rears up to torment him anew. His bitter struggle is enacted in condensed form in the overture, which begins with the 'Pilgrims' Chorus' representing the side of virtue and religion. A grave and reverent beauty sounds through each chord of this penitential hymn.

'Pilgrims' Chorus' and Venus motive from *Tannhäuser*

No sooner have these strains died away than the sensuous sounds depicting Venus and her court of love soar through the orchestra.

(ii)

So Wagner leads us on through the drama of his agonized knight until we know by the brilliant and fervent return of the Pilgrims' music that good has won the knight's soul at last.

One major problem confronted all the singers: they had to master the new type of vocal line that Wagner was evolving to go with his continuous orchestral symphony. They were used to clearly divided recitatives and arias, and were all at sea when it came to lyrical 'endless melody' which

... divisions. It took Wagner years to educate singers out of their old habits and into the new techniques he required, but his success with one or two of the first *Tannhäuser* cast showed him it could be done.

The scenery ordered from Paris was late, and the Hall of Song did not arrive at all until after 19th October, the first night: the throne room made for Weber's *Oberon* had to be used instead. The first audience was quite appreciative, but the critics tore *Tannhäuser* to pieces next day. Wagner cut the parts that Tichatschek had badly misinterpreted and waited for the second performance. It was poorly attended but enthusiastically received. The third performance was acclaimed by a full house: *Tannhäuser* was established.

On Palm Sunday 1846, Wagner conducted Beethoven's Ninth Symphony at an annual concert. This work so dear to his heart was at that time almost unknown in Dresden and the court officials doubted if it would attract an audience at all. To prove them wrong, Wagner rallied his supporters and a capacity audience gathered to hear his superb performance. It was this symphony with its final outburst of exultant song that Wagner recognized as the forebear of his own symphonic operas. By popular request the work was repeated the following year.

About this time a financial crisis occurred. Schröder-Devrient was jealous of young Johanna and began to suspect Wagner of bringing this gifted and beautiful relative to Dresden to take her place. To have her revenge she placed Wagner's IOU for the loan of four years earlier in the hands of her lawyer, who promptly sued him. Wagner had no choice but to make a clean breast of his position to Baron von Lüttichau, the director of the theatre, and beg him for a royal loan. Five thousand thalers, three-and-a-half times Wagner's annual salary, was granted him—a sum that would take a prudent lifetime to repay. Anxiety over this matter left him in poor health and the management gave him three months' leave. He went to the country with Minna and the dog of the moment and began to compose *Lohengrin*.

The main event of the winter was a production of Gluck's *Iphigenia in Aulis* in a new revised version by Wagner. His sympathy with the earlier opera reformer was apparent at every turn of the score, and even the press sang his praises. His own reforming zeal suffered a rebuff when a carefully thought-out report on how the orchestra could be better run was returned to him and all his eminently sensible suggestions rejected. After that he refused to attend theatre committee meetings since the members only seemed interested in trivial issues.

The following autumn he took two months' leave to conduct a few performances of *Rienzi* in Berlin. The court of the King of Prussia was there, and being desperate for money Wagner hoped to persuade the monarch to command further performances of his works, but all in vain. When he got back to Dresden he had to ask Lüttichau for a rise in salary, and was sorely humiliated to read the Baron's memo to the King on the subject. It stated that Wagner was in grave financial difficulties over the recent publication of some of his works. His ideas, it said, were too exalted, and he deluded himself in thinking his operas the equal of Meyerbeer's. It might be as well to dismiss him, though he had done one or two redeeming things such as *Iphigenia*. Perhaps this time he should be granted the necessary money to sort out his affairs and threatened with instant dismissal should he accumulate any further debts.

That he got the money was beside the point, but that he, Wagner, a great artist, should be spoken of thus by a puffed-up pawn of the court was insufferable. In the spring of 1848 he drew up another radical document, 'Plan for the organisation of a German National Theatre for the Kingdom of Saxony'. The plan would take the theatre out of the court's hands and entrust its running to a national union of informed dramatists and composers, much better equipped for the job than mere courtiers. The King would remain national head, but the director would be an artist— the royal conductor, and not 'a mere court placeman with no qualifications whatever for the task'. Standards would be improved; a national music school would be founded to train artists; there would be five performances a week instead of seven; the lot of chorus singers and orchestral players would be improved. The plan was submitted to various ministers of state, who politely rejected it. Wagner had tried, and failed, to bring about reform through peaceful means. Now he lent an ear to those who said that revolution alone could bring change.

The French overthrew their king again in February 1848, a revolt that spread like wildfire to Germany where the people were ruled by absolute princes. The French were fighting for better social conditions and fairer representation in Parliament—rights denied to Germans also. How could Wagner go on creating music when the land to which he gave it was so unenlightened? He would fight, if necessary, for a brave new Utopia for his music. He would have been happy to reform just a microcosm, Dresden's Royal Theatre, but since that was denied him he must join the wider battlefield. He joined an extremist political club, the *Vaterlands-Verein*, and in June delivered a rousing speech, supporting the King but decrying the obsolete institutions and fawning officials that hindered his just rule. The incredible spectacle of the royal conductor uttering such sentiments caused a marvellous scandal in Dresden, and Wagner had to withdraw to Vienna for a month while the furore died down. Afterwards he resumed his conducting as conscientiously as ever. To support his socialist dreams of abolishing the aristocracy and the capitalist system, he devised an opera plot on just such themes, drawing on the great *Nibelungen* legend. Like Siegfried, its hero, he was a crusader in a hostile, corrupt world. The opera was to be called *Siegfried's Death* at that time, but later became known to the world as *Götter-dämmerung* (*The Twilight of the Gods*). He planned it for some stage of the future, not for Dresden, where in autumn *Lohengrin* was turned down because of his official disfavour.

Matters deteriorated further during the winter: a revival of *The Flying Dutchman* was cancelled, and petty royal complaints about his conducting were made. He plotted an opera about another lonely revolutionary, *Jesus of Nazareth*, and then abandoned it. He contributed articles to revolutionary newspapers. Day by day political catastrophe drew nearer. His future at Dresden seemed so uncertain that he was content to give himself up to the stream of events. Shortly before the storm broke, Liszt wrote to say he had given two performances of *Tannhäuser* at Weimar with no small success. Could Wagner attend the third? A week's leave in May 1849 was duly granted: but Wagner never returned, for by the time he reached Weimar, he was a wanted man.

The first days of May brought open war to Dresden. Wagner's employer, the Saxon king, refused to enforce the new liberal constitution demanded by the revolutionary Frankfurt Parliament, and called in Prussian troops to back him up. The Dresden rebels were ready for a fight and engaged the unwelcome Prussian soldiers in civil war. Before this onslaught Wagner distributed propaganda leaflets around the town, asking, 'Are you on our side against the foreign troops?' From the high belfry of the Kreuz Church he watched the action day and night, and surveyed the wrecked and barricaded streets of Dresden. When the rebel leaders withdrew to the country a few days later, Wagner went with them. He arrived after the others and put up at a different hotel. Had he been with them, he, too, would have been arrested for treason that night. Somehow he fled to Weimar where Liszt protected him and planned his hasty escape from Germany. A reproachful Minna came to bid him farewell. She could not forgive him for throwing away the fine social position that meant everything to her, and so he went into exile alone. Liszt gave him money, a passport, and instructions to travel to Switzerland, and then to Paris. By the 28th May he was on Swiss oil, safe, well, and rejoicing in a freedom he had not known for years.

VI

The Musician of the Future

After a few days in Zürich he set off by coach for Paris. Liszt wanted him to write a new work for the Opéra and to get *Rienzi* put on there too; but neither project could keep Wagner in Paris for long. His bitter memories of the place revived, and back he went to Zürich. When he had a suitable new work ready, he assured Liszt, he would try his luck in France again, but in the meantime he would make his home in peaceful Switzerland.

For the next four years of his life there he wrote no music. Instead, volume after volume of prose flowed from his pen. All the theories and ideals that had been boiling away inside him in Dresden now found expression on paper. First came a pamphlet called *Art and Revolution* in which he compared the degenerate artistic scene of modern Germany with the glorious one of ancient Greece. While all classes of people had gathered for the Greek tragedies, only the well-to-do attended German theatres. To the Greeks, theatre-going was almost a religious ritual: to the Germans, a money-making entertainment for bored, tired minds. The Greek drama expressed the unity of the nation by combining all its arts in one: rhetoric, sculpture, painting and music were all involved. But when disunity came to the Greek people, the drama split up into its component parts and each art stood alone. The great 'unified art-work' was lost to the world, never to be reborn —unless 'the great revolution of mankind' could re-create it. The new man-kind must be free of greed and sophistication, and of bondage to the god of gold. When wealth no longer divided the German nation, a united people would once more express itself in a united art-work. Such was Wagner's dream. Because of the notoriety attached to his name in Germany, people quickly snapped up the pamphlet and it was soon in its second edition.

While he lived in increasing poverty in Zürich, he envisaged the new world where he would bring forth the great unified art-work. *The Art-Work of the Future*, written in October 1849, tells of poetry, pictures, sculpture and

46

music giving up their individual identities and combining in the complete art-work. As Wagner was none too fond of the arts other than music he did not mind denying them a separate life in the future. Painting beautiful scenery would occupy the artist, and planning statuesque movement the sculptor. When men no longer acted as selfish units but gave themselves up to the community, then they would want the arts to do the same, making one communal art for all to share together.

Having worked all this out of his system for the time being, he started on a new opera called *Wieland the Smith*. Minna had rejoined him in the autumn and was constantly nagging him to write something for Paris. Liszt added his voice to hers and in January 1850 they persuaded him to try selling *Wieland* in Paris. He went, knowing in his heart what they failed to understand: that a solid Teuton like Wieland could have no appeal for superficial Parisians, nor a music-drama succeed in the greatest stronghold of old-fashioned opera. The Parisian operatic rat-race was totally abhorrent to him: he neither expected nor wanted to triumph there. He felt ill. There was nothing he could do in Paris. A promised performance of the *Tannhäuser* Overture fell through when the orchestral parts failed to arrive. He was sickened by a performance of Meyerbeer's *The Prophet* at the Opéra; to Wagner it was no more than a hollow confidence trick, and Paris blindly adored it. Frustrated and nearing his wits' end, he abandoned *Wieland* and fell into the arms of a beautiful English woman.

Jessie Thomas was married to a Bordeaux wine merchant, Laussot, and had met Wagner briefly in Dresden. Together with another Dresden lady, Frau Ritter, she now proposed to support him to the extent of 3,000 francs a year, and asked him down to Bordeaux for a holiday. The idea of being financed by wealthy admirers seemed right and proper to Wagner, but it offended Minna's bourgeois sensibilities. She could not live on 'alms' from another woman. Tired of her lack of understanding Wagner accepted the Laussot's holiday invitation. He found Jessie intelligent, musical and highly appreciative of his genius—all the things that Minna was not. Drawn closer and closer by days of music-making and deep conversation, they fell in love.

Three weeks passed, then Wagner returned to Paris to think things over. He decided he would leave Europe and go with Jessie to Greece or Asia Minor and forget his tangled career. On 17th April he told Minna by letter that he was leaving her. Then the melodrama began. Minna hurried to Paris in search of him—and he fled to Geneva to avoid her. Jessie blurted out the secret affair to her mother, who informed Laussot: he determined to shoot Wagner. The latter hastened to Bordeaux to make his peace, only to be ordered out of the town by the police. Back in Geneva, Frau Ritter came specially from Dresden to cheer him, but there the affair ended, for Jessie's family made her repent of her misdeeds, promise to see him no more and burn his letters. He felt more dead than alive as he wrote to Frau Ritter, 'Never will I be ashamed of this love: if it has died, if . . . it can never come to life again, yet was its kiss the richest delight of my life. Not honour, nor splendour, nor fame will ever outweigh it for me.' Minna pathetically begged him to come home, and as he felt almost as sorry for her as for himself, he duly did so. The Jessie episode was forgotten and domestic harmony restored.

It was now a full two years since the completion of *Lohengrin* and still no performance had taken place. There was only one man who could, and would, bring it before the world: Liszt. His decision to stage *Lohengrin* at Weimar was a bold one. Of all Wagner's music-dramas so far it was the one farthest removed from traditional opera, and the heaviest in its demands on singers, orchestra and staging. The performance took place in August 1850. Wagner of course could not enter Germany to hear it, but was pleased enough with its effects. When other little German companies saw that a Wagner work *could* be done successfully in a small theatre, all their previous nervousness departed, and soon the music-dramas were staged all over the country.

In Zürich Wagner was treated as the local celebrity. He was invited to conduct special symphony concerts and gala opera nights. Whenever he appeared there were high prices and packed houses. He refused to become musical director of the opera-house but agreed to train two young friends of his from Dresden in that role. They were Karl Ritter, son of his benefactress, and Hans von Bülow. Though Hans conducted well, Karl was so bad that Wagner often had to take his place, much to the delight of public and performers. In the end the demand became so heavy that he had to give up these opera appearances altogether.

All through the winter of 1850–1 he was busy with a lengthy prose work called *Opera and Drama*. When it was finished he read it in public over twelve evenings. Interest in the readings grew so rapidly that by the end he had to hire a large hall to accommodate all the eager listeners. He explained to them that modern opera had become little more than a concert in costume, an excuse for virtuoso singers to show off their brilliant technique. The drama was forgotten amid this welter of showy sound, and indeed few people cared at all about the content of the plot: it was just a pretext for music. Things were quite the reverse when the ancient Greeks combined drama and music. Then, the drama was all important, and music was its servant. The art-work of the future would be like that too. Its subjects would not be petty or frivolous, but lofty and universal. The most sublime of feelings and emotions would be contained in the poem, and then expanded by the music, for music can often say deeper things than words alone. In most of the current operas the orchestra was only there to provide a support for the singers, but the orchestra of the future would learn to share in the drama. It would have a self-sufficient part all of its own, on the surface of which the voice part would be borne along 'as a boat on water'. The orchestra's role would be to 'explain' the drama on stage, by recalling earlier music and past emotions, and giving premonitions of what was to come, thus revealing a good deal more about a character and his thoughts than he needs to say. The return of the principal motives at the drama's behest would bind the whole work together into a seamless tissue.

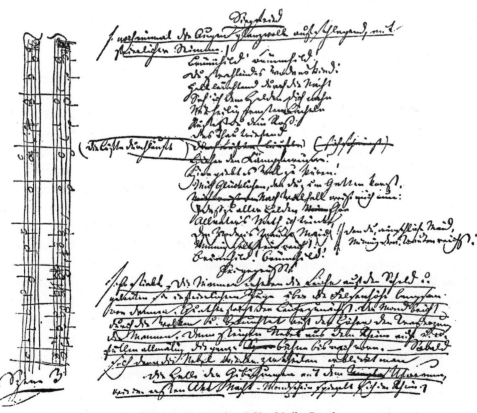

Wagner's sketch of *Siegfried's Death*

Before long Wagner's audience discovered that the readings from *Opera and Drama* were preparing them for his next music-drama; he read them *Siegfried's Death* soon after. The hugeness of its scope was beginning to worry him. He could not imagine the mighty downfall of the gods being adequately presented on Weimar's tiny stage, so he proposed to write a less mammoth work about the younger Siegfried. In the course of the year this plan took a staggering new turn. Not only would he write *both* dramas about Siegfried, 'the man we wait and wish for', but would dramatize the earlier part of the *Nibelungen* legend, before Siegfried comes on to the scene. *The Valkyrie* would present the old regime of the gods, to be destroyed by the coming hero, and *The Rhinegold* reveal the origin of the cursed gold ring that dominates the whole saga. His intention to write something more for Weimar was forgotten. This huge epic cycle, *The Ring*, would be presented some day at a special festival, in a special theatre, over a period of four days.

All through 1852 he worked on the four books. Thanks to Frau Ritter's allowance and royalties from performances of his works, he had the freedom to write just when he pleased. He took time off to go on long mountaineering tours, and an eccentric water-cure from which he returned ill, emaciated, and a fanatical teetotaller. He was in a constant state of nervous anxiety, tormented by doubts that his great *Ring* festival could ever become reality.

A Wagner festival of sorts was held in Zürich in May 1853, during the week of his fortieth birthday. Specially invited players came from all over Germany to take part. For half the week they rehearsed strenuously and then gave three triumphant concerts of extracts from his operas. He gave public readings of the poems during the week so that the concert-goers should know the meaning of the music. The whole affair was a tremendous success. After the last concert banquets were given for him, a poem read in his honour and a laurel wreath and silver goblet presented to him. Requests for repeat performances poured in from all over Switzerland. But Wagner was not a happy man. His exile distressed him deeply, especially as he was powerless to exercise any form of control over the way his works were being performed in Germany. He was too disturbed to compose, though the books of the *Ring* were ready and waiting. He could not bring himself to begin after so long a silence. What if his gift had disappeared?

He went to St. Moritz for a nerve treatment and then to Italy in search of the right environment for creation. In the course of the holiday he caught dysentery. Feeling wretched he dragged himself out for a country walk one day and returned to his hotel room quite exhausted. He stretched himself out on the sofa, but instead of going to sleep, 'fell into a kind of somnolent state' in which he suddenly felt as if he were drowning in a great flood of water. 'The rushing sound formed itself in my brain into a musical sound, the chord of E♭ major, which continually re-echoed in broken forms; these broken chords seemed to be melodic passages of increasing motion, yet the pure triad of E♭ major never changed. . . . I awoke from my half-sleep in terror, feeling as though the waves were rushing high over my head.' At once he knew that this was the orchestral prelude to *The Rhinegold*, the very music to express the motion of the Rhine, under whose waters the drama begins. He telegraphed Minna to prepare his study hastily, for he was coming home at once to start work.

Opening motive from *The Rhinegold* and its progression

VII

Tristan

Within a year, *The Rhinegold* and *The Valkyrie* were all but finished, in spite of many incidental worries. The money problem was larger than ever, since he had reached a stage where luxury was an absolute prerequisite to composing. He needed to isolate himself in densely carpeted rooms hung with heavy curtains and costly draperies. His clothes had to be of the softest silk so as not to irritate the skin complain to which he was often prone. All this luxury gave rise to much idle talk in Zürich, for though his Dresden creditors were at the door, he refused to deny himself anything. Fortunately, several rich men of Zürich shared his conviction that it was their duty to support him. Otto Wesendonck was the kindest of all; after knowing Wagner only a year, he was paying off huge debts on his behalf. Wagner repaid him by forming a strong attachment for his beautiful wife, Mathilde.

Minna's health was another source of concern as she had developed symptoms of heart disease: no doubt the cares of being Wagner's wife were a strong contributory factor. As her illness made her more irritable and irrational towards him, so he retreated to an intellectual plane where she could not follow. He read *The World as Will and Idea* by the philosopher Schopenhauer, and was amazed to find that it crystallized his own pessimistic creed. Schopenhauer believed in life as endless desire that only death could satisfy: only surrender of the will to live, he said, could redeem the individual from the yearning dreams and illusions of this false world. That Wagner had a strong death-wish is clear from this letter to Liszt: 'When the storms of life rise to the power of a hurricane, I find a last anodyne that alone brings me sleep in wakeful nights—the profound longing of my heart for death, complete unconsciousness, total nihility, a final end to dreaming, the last and only salvation.'

At the end of 1854 he told Liszt of a new work that in his present mood he must write. It was *Tristan and Isolde,* an old Cornish legend of desire brought about by a love potion. In Wagner's hands it was to become a tragedy of yearning so intense that death alone could resolve it. 'Since I have never enjoyed in life the real happiness of love,' he wrote, 'I will erect to this most beautiful of all dreams a memorial in which, from beginning to end, this love shall for once drink its fill.' Under cover of this passionate tale he would live out his frustrated love for Otto Wesendonck's wife, Mathilde. Otto was the King Mark of the story, who as Isolde's husband stood between the love-lorn pair. The idea grew in him for three years before he finally put aside *The Ring* for its sake.

A surprise letter from the London Philharmonic Society reached Wagner early in 1855. As a result, he paid a four-month visit to London to conduct a season of concerts. It was an unhappy experience. A hostile press was ready and waiting, incensed by the anti-Semitic things he had written in a recent pamphlet called *Judaism in Music*. Many of the critics were Jews themselves, and even those who were not, supported Mendelssohn, a Jew and the darling of English music. Wagner was convinced the whole press was in the pay of Meyerbeer, by now his arch-enemy. Mendelssohn had accustomed the public to some very strange tempi in Beethoven's symphonies, which Wagner naturally corrected—only to be accused of misinterpretation. His expressive style of conducting was frowned upon too by those whose criterion was the Mendelssohnian strict 'beat'.

He found the orchestra good but complacent, and unwilling to grant him the numerous rehearsals he demanded : one per concert was considered ample. The programmes were inordinately lengthy. English audiences liked to hear at least two symphonies, a concerto, two or three overtures and several vocal solos all at one sitting. Wagner was exasperated at the way they received each item with equal enthusiasm, be it a paltry song, inferior overture or miraculous symphony. He was also bemused by the interminable oratorio performances through which the English solemnly sat, clasping their piano scores like prayer books. The London fogs made him ill. 'I live like a damned soul in hell,' he wrote to Liszt. The fact that he spoke no English added to his difficulties, but he did muster up enough French to converse pleasurably with Berlioz who was also on a conducting visit. Queen Victoria and Prince Albert attended one of his concerts and commanded a special performance of the *Tannhäuser* Overture; but even the stamp of royal approval could not dispel his disagreeable impressions of England.

After-effects in the way of depressing ill health dogged him for some time after his return to Zürich. Tichatschek came to visit him in summer 1856 and found him in the midst of a painful bout of his skin disease. Happily it was cured later in the year and did not recur until twenty-three years later. In September he started work on *Siegfried* in spite of the distracting noises of his flautist and pianist neighbours. The tinkering of a neighbouring tinsmith was a further annoyance, but he was pleased when the noise suggested suitable 'hammering' music for Mime's forge. He was preoccupied with cares—about his health and Minna's; Otto and Mathilde; and, of course, money, for even friendly Swiss bankers had bottoms to their pockets. He brooded on Schopenhauer, *Tristan* and Buddhism. In February 1857 Otto brought him joy by offering him, at a nominal rent, a peaceful little house called the *Asyl* in the grounds of his own lakeside villa. In April he and Minna moved in. The close proximity of Mathilde was disturbing: in the summer he broke off *Siegfried* at the end of Act Two and began *Tristan*. 'I have led my young Siegfried into the beautiful forest solitude,' he told Liszt. 'There I have left him under a linden tree, and with tears from the depths of my heart, said farewell to him.'

Tristan was intended as an easily performable work for the smaller theatres. Over *The Ring* he was temporarily in despair: various Grand Dukes had expressed interest in buying the end-product but none would support him while he wrote it. It might be years before it was complete, and meanwhile the world would know nothing of the new, mature Wagner, the musician of the future. His last work, *Lohengrin*, was ten years old, and he had travelled far since its birth. While the first act of *Tristan* was in progress, Hans von Bülow and his new young wife, Cosima, one of Liszt's daughters, came to stay with him. 'I can think of nothing more calculated to bring me a sense of blessing and refreshment than to be with this glorious, unique man, whom one must venerate like a god. In the presence of this Great and Good all the *misère* of life melts away, I rise above it,' wrote Hans, the devoted Wagnerian.

The Prelude and First Act were finished by the end of the year. No one had ever tried to express such fierce yearning in music before, and Wagner had to find a new kind of musical language for it. The very first bars of the Prelude reveal the method he used. Each chord there is an unresolved dissonance whose poignant sound finds no longed-for resolution in the chord that follows.

Tristan

Opening of the Prelude from *Tristan and Isolde*

Such continuous discords were unheard of when Wagner wrote them, and revolutionary in their effect on music. Since then, people have come to accept that dissonance can be beautiful, and that music need not be in any particular key. Wagner used some of the *Tristan* music in settings of five love poems by Mathilde which he composed in the winter of 1857–8. He scored one of them for small orchestra and had it performed under her window on her birthday just before Christmas. Here is the last song, 'Träume' (Dreams). Wagner introduces some of his 'yearning' harmonies from the fifth bar onwards. The vocal phrases, full of restless dotted rhythms, often start in one key and finish in another, adding to the sense of longing and incompleteness. As the words become increasingly passionate in the middle of the song the voice part grows more striving and continuous. It has scarcely any cadences or points of rest, and it is by avoiding them that Wagner makes his melodies sound 'endless'.

The *Wesendonck Lieder*: 'Träume'

dolcissimo

un poco cresc.

dim.

p

Sag', welch wun-der-ba — re Träu — — me
Say, oh say what won - d'rous dream — — ings

pp

hal - ten mei- nen Sinn ump- fan - - gen,
keep my in-most soul re-volv - - ing,

dass sie nicht wie lee - - re Schäu - - me sind in
that they not like emp - ty gleam - - ings in - to

ö - des Nichts ver - gan - gen? Träu - - me, die in
noth-ing are dis - solv - ing? Dream - - ings, that with

p

je - der Stun - de, je - dem Ta - ge schö - ner blüh'n, und mit ih- rer
ev - ery hour,— ev - ery day in bright - ness grow, and with their ce -

poco cresc.

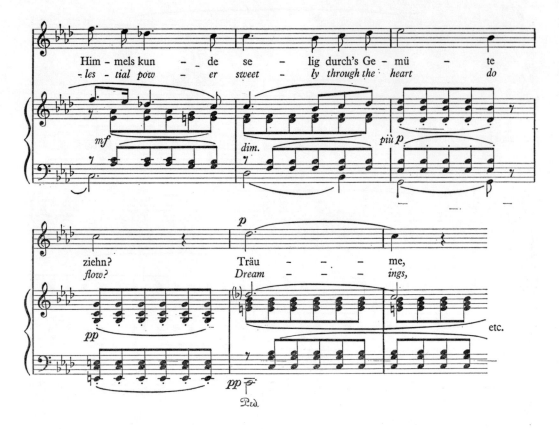

Him - mels kun — de se - lig durch's Ge - mü - te
- les - tial pow — er sweet - ly through the heart do

ziehn? Träu - - - me,
flow? Dream - - - ings,

The situation between the Wagners and the Wesendoncks grew more and more tense until one day it reached breaking point. On the 7th April 1858 Minna intercepted a secret letter from her husband to Mathilde. Predictably, she saw it as evidence of a bourgeois 'affair'. It was useless to protest the innocence of his love, impossible to explain to Minna about lofty, spiritual bonds. In the role of wronged wife she showed the offending letter to Mathilde and threatened to expose her to Otto. The noble Otto had always been aware of the fine-spun love between Mathilde and Richard and nevertheless had continued faithful husband to the one and generous benefactor to the other. Minna's plebeian outburst shattered the ideality of the triangle and Wagner knew his days at the *Asyl* were numbered.

He sent Minna away for a badly-needed heart cure and in her three months' absence gladly lost himself in the second act of *Tristan*. When she returned in July, Tichatschek and the von Bülows were visiting at the *Asyl*. The young couple witnessed a horrible scene between Minna and Wagner on the very day of their arrival: Minna had delivered another insult to Mathilde, making it impossible for them to go on living in Otto's property.

Tristan

A servant had erected a floral arch to celebrate Minna's return and Minna had insisted on its remaining up for a number of days to show Mathilde that triumph, and not humiliation, surrounded her homecoming. Mathilde protested strongly against this crude and petty gesture, and Wagner could see that the situation was beyond repair.

A month later he left the *Asyl* for ever. Minna went to Saxony and he to Venice. He rented stately rooms in an old palace on the Grand Canal and decorated them with rich red draperies. He found peace at last. His life was quiet and ordered: in the mornings he would work at *Tristan*, then drift down the Canal by gondola to meet Karl Ritter for lunch. After a walk he

Wagner composing

would return home along the Canal and do some more work before Karl joined him for the evening. He kept a finely-worded diary for Mathilde and wrote prosaic letters to Minna. Seven months later the second act of *Tristan* was finished. The question then arose as to where he could go to compose Act Three. Venice in the summer would be too hot for his delicate health—besides which, the water disagreed with him and he missed his climbing excursions in the Swiss mountains. In addition, the authorities made it clear that they had no wish to harbour a Saxon exile indefinitely— so in March 1859, Wagner moved on to Lucerne.

As it was early in the season, he managed to get a whole floor of the Hotel Schweizerhof to himself. His grand piano followed him from Venice and Act Three was begun. The infinite sadness of its subject put him in a mood of deepest melancholy which prevailed for most of his six months in Lucerne. His courtesy visits to the Wesendoncks were gloomy occasions, intended only to quieten the wagging tongues of those who speculated on the Wagners' sudden departure from Zürich. Each morning he went for a ride on an aged horse named Lise which turned back regularly at fixed spots, regardless of Wagner's directions. So the months passed, and by August, *Tristan*, his 'child of sorrow' was complete. Now he no longer needed cloistered seclusion, but a cosy home where Minna could look after him, in a town where he could hear good music—his own included. Otto Wesendonck's unfailing generosity made this next move possible, as he paid Wagner handsomely for the publishing rights in *The Ring*. In September 1859, twenty years after his first disastrous sojourn there, Wagner went back to live in Paris.

VIII

Return to Paris

His Paris household included a manservant for himself and a lady's maid for the ailing Minna, who joined him in November. Neither servant endured the lash of her caustic tongue for long. Wagner could well have done without the renewal of domestic warfare for he had troubles enough outside his home. *Tristan* had been in rehearsal at the theatre in Karlsruhe since autumn, but the bemused singers first floundered and now sank. Wagner reflected bitterly that they would have stayed afloat if only he had been able to supervise the proceedings himself. Now there was no alternative but to present his new works in Paris—hardly the soundest of Wagnerian strongholds.

All thoughts of resuming *The Ring* were abandoned as he plunged once more into the thick of theatrical affairs. He planned to invite the best German singers he knew to come and found a German theatre, where *Tannhäuser* and then *Lohengrin* could lead up to *Tristan*. Before the scheme got under way he thought it wise to initiate Parisians with a few introductory concerts which were duly given at the beginning of 1860. Neither he nor his campaigners bargained for the incredible hostility of the press. From the safe distance of Berlin, Meyerbeer bribed the critics to pour scorn on the concerts. Their unanimous derision caused a sensation that unexpectedly rallied many outraged and fanatical supporters to Wagner's side. The poet Baudelaire was one of them. After the final concert he wrote to Wagner: 'I am of an age at which one no longer amuses oneself by writing to eminent men; and I should have hesitated for a long time to send you a letter expressive of admiration if my eyes did not light, day after day, on absurd and shameful articles in which every possible attempt is made to defame your genius. . . . In the end, my indignation has driven me to testify to you my gratitude: I said to myself, "I want to mark myself off from all these imbeciles!" ' Baudelaire and other fervent admirers, like the young Saint-Saëns, became regular guests at Wagner's Wednesday evening 'at homes'.

Return to Paris

The German theatre idea fell apart after the failure of the concerts: but royal sympathy was roused, and in March, no less a person than the Emperor of France, Napoleon III, commanded a production of *Tannhäuser* at the Opéra. Pauline Metternich, an Austrian princess in the thick of Parisian court life, had persuaded him to help Wagner in this way. He received the news with mixed feelings. 'God knows what will come of this projected *Tannhäuser*,' he wrote to Liszt, 'inwardly I have no faith in it, and that for good reasons.' The manager of the Opéra wanted him to make alterations in concession to Parisian taste, and specially urged the addition of a lengthy grand ballet to the second act. Wagner had no intention of disrupting his dramatic scheme to please Paris, and said so—though to please himself he did rewrite the Venus scene in Act One to include a wild ballet-like orgy.

In the summer came news he had awaited for eleven long years. Thanks to the intervention of a Prussian princess, the Saxon king had agreed to let Wagner re-enter any part of Germany but Saxony itself. In August he went to thank the princess and collect Minna from one of her heart cures. He felt curiously little emotion at treading German soil again. When he got back to Paris, *Tannhäuser* rehearsals began. An outstanding German tenor, Albert Niemann, had been engaged for the title role, and of all the cast it was this one German who caused him sorrow. As rehearsals progressed Niemann heard from journalist acquaintances of a plot afoot to ruin both Wagner and *Tannhäuser*. Since he was only interested in his own personal success in Paris and cared nothing for Wagner's, he simply stopped trying when he heard of *Tannhäuser*'s pending doom. He ignored all Wagner's directions and fell back on his usual stagey interpretation of the part. Niemann excepted, the cast shaped up well.

There was a strange rule at the Opéra that forbade composers to conduct their own works, so about three weeks before the first performance, Wagner handed over his baton to Dietsch,[1] the regular *chef d'orchestre*. Dietsch's conducting, from a first violin part and giving no leads, quickly reduced *Tannhäuser* to 'a colourless chaos'. Wagner tried to cancel the production but it was too late: a great deal of money had been spent on the endless rehearsals, and on the sumptuous costumes and scenery. Paris audiences were not accustomed to Wagnerian standards of excellence, so the first performance, on 13th March 1861, did not strike them as being below par. On the whole, it was quite a success. There were a few outbursts of whistling and shouting, but the applause was louder than the boos.

[1] The very man who set Wagner's one-act *Flying Dutchman* plot to music in 1842

It was on the second night that bedlam broke loose. Act One went by without interruption, then in Act Two, the young nobles of the Jockey Club began their demonstration. It was for their benefit that all works staged at the Opéra had a ballet in the second act, for these playboy aristocrats never took their seats before ten o'clock when they had finished wining and dining. The sole reason they came at all was to see their mistresses dance. They were incensed at Wagner's denial of their noble whims and determined to wreck the proceedings, in spite of the Emperor's attempts to bargain with them. They kept up an incessant racket with their dog whistles till the very

Wagner marches against Paris

end, only momentarily silenced by surprise when Niemann flung his pilgrim's hat at them in the third act. Wagner did not even bother to attend the next performance. Instead he stayed at home with Minna, smoking and drinking tea. At the theatre the pandemonium was worse than before as the Jockeys were in their seats right from the start. Police lined the corridors to protect the noble gentlemen from the indignant public. Fights broke out; the performance stopped and started; the audience screamed abuse at the Jockeys; they whistled all the louder—and the music was drowned and ruined. The management now acceded to Wagner's repeated wish that *Tannhäuser* be withdrawn. All he salvaged from the ruin was a paltry 750 francs, royalties for the three performances. He gave it all to the impoverished man who translated the libretto into French.

Return to Paris

Once more, scandalized supporters flew to Wagner's side. Baudelaire wrote his great article *Richard Wagner et* Tannhäuser *à Paris*. There was talk of performances in other Parisian theatres, even plans among rich men to found a *Théâtre Wagner* there. In Germany where *Tannhäuser* was very popular, there was an indignant wave of partisanship. Riding on its crest Wagner visited Karlsruhe in April and the Grand Duke agreed to the salvaging of the sunken *Tristan*. This time, Wagner was at liberty to supervise the rehearsals himself. He went to Vienna to engage suitable singers, and while he was there saw *Lohengrin* for the first time, perfectly performed. The manager of the Opera was reluctant to let his singers go to Karlsruhe, but suggested that since Wagner was so moved by Vienna's *Lohengrin*, he should bring *Tristan* to life there too. So Wagner made his apologies to the Grand Duke of Baden, and looked forward to an ideal production at the Imperial Viennese Opera House.

He returned to Paris to tidy up his affairs. Minna supervised the storing of their furniture, then left for a cure. Until his own departure in July, Wagner was the guest of the Prussian Embassy. In those last days he wrote a short 'thank-you' piece, the *Album Piece in C*, for his friend Princess Metternich. She had suffered the scorn of press and royalty alike for championing his cause. The piece was exactly the sort of thing that grand ladies of the day liked to play when guests came for a musical evening in the *salon*. The melody, just a little sentimental, is elaborated in an affecting way, but not so much as to make it difficult to perform.

Album Piece in C for piano

E

Back in Vienna he found all was not well with *Tristan*. Ander, the tenor, kept losing his voice—partly from terror at the enormity of his part. Wagner's enemies spread the lie that the work was unperformable. The production date receded into the distance, and so did Wagner's fee. Once more he was penniless. He went to see his publisher, Schott, in December, and came away with the fine sum of 10,000 francs: advance payment for *The Mastersingers*. He left *Tristan* to its fate in Vienna and went back to Paris to write the poem, basing it on the original one he had drafted at Marienbad in 1845.

The question of somewhere congenial to settle down now arose. None of his friends could offer him a permanent home, so he chose Biebrich, a town on the Rhine that was conveniently placed for all the big cities, and moved into a flat there in February 1862. Minna came to visit him for 'ten atrocious days' and nearly drove him mad with her wild accusations and bitter reproaches. She was living in Dresden and was working hard on the authorities to allow Wagner's re-entry into Saxony. She could not bear to let him live happily away from her: he must be captive at her side. The full pardon was granted at the end of March, but he did not return to Dresden. He knew that for the sake of his music and Minna's heart, their separation must be permanent. He went to visit her just once, later in the year, but never saw her again after that. She died in January 1866.

He was soon engrossed in *The Mastersingers*. The von Bülows came to visit him in the midst of Act One, and by the end of their stay his growing conviction that Cosima belonged to him had become a certainty in his mind. By the autumn he was compelled to make some money by taking up his baton again in various towns. His Leipzig concert included the first performance of the Prelude to *The Mastersingers*. Vienna heard selections from *The Ring* for the first time, including the thrilling 'Ride of the Valkyries' (the warrior maidens of Valhalla). Prague received him with wild enthusiasm, and in St. Petersburg and Moscow he was honoured by the nobility and invited to read *The Ring* at courtly tea-parties.

Meanwhile in Vienna *Tristan* had almost ground to a halt. He decided he would simply have to go and live there, so in May 1863 he left his Biebrich lodgings and settled in the Viennese suburb of Penzing. There his hard-earned concert fees quickly flowed through his fingers. His house was palatial; he had two servants and an excellent wine cellar, but his presence did nothing to help *Tristan*. Ander became increasingly nervous about his part, and infected the Isolde, Frau Dustmann. Everyone concerned regarded the project with total pessimism. Wagner busied himself with the new work and wondered where his next money would come from.

Ludwig II of Bavaria

Neuschwanstein Castle which was built
for Ludwig II between 1869 and 1886

A scene from the first performance of *Tristan and
Isolde*. Malvina and Ludwig Schnorr von Carolsfeld in the title roles

Act II of Wieland Wagner's 1962
production of *Tristan and Isolde*

An engraving of the Bayreuth Festival Theatre shortly before it was officially opened
for the first performance of *The Ring*

A recent photograph of the Festival Theatre

He gave more concerts, in Budapest and several German towns. Supporting two households, his own and Minna's, was desperately difficult on an irregular income, but he never failed to provide for her. By the start of 1864 he had to resort to money-lenders. His debts increased daily and he could not meet them. In March, not for the first time in his life, he fled from his threatening creditors. He headed for Switzerland, and on his way passed through Munich, the Bavarian capital, a city in mourning for its late king, Maximilian II. In a shop window Wagner saw a striking photograph of the new monarch, Ludwig II, a handsome eighteen-year-old.

The Wesendoncks were not prepared to fend for Wagner this time, so he went to stay with the Wille family whose lovely country estate near Zürich used to be a favourite visiting place of his. Frau Wille did her best to cheer him up, but he was sorely depressed and embittered. At the height of his career he was in the depths of despair. 'A *light* must show itself,' he wrote to Peter Cornelius, the composer, 'a *man* must arise who will help me vigorously *now*.'

In April he went to Stuttgart in a futile attempt to get *Tristan* produced. One night while he was out visiting there, a card was brought to him. It bore the inscription 'Secretary to the King of Bavaria'. Wagner was afraid it might be some creditor trying to trick him, so sent word that he was not present. He returned to his hotel and found that the caller had been looking for him there too. He was coming again at ten the next morning. Wagner spent a restless night dreaming of new disasters—but all was well. 'The light' was shining, 'the man' had arisen.

IX

King Ludwig to the Rescue

Ever since young King Ludwig had given the order 'Find Richard Wagner for me', Herr Pfistermeister, his secretary, had been pursuing the fugitive composer from town to town. At last he had found him, and at the appointed hour presented himself in Wagner's hotel room. Gifts from the King, a ring and a portrait, were handed over and the unbelievable royal summons given: Wagner was to go to Munich at once. Everything he could possibly want would be placed at his disposal, *The Ring* would be produced and King Ludwig would be his friend and protector for evermore.

In 1863 Wagner had published the *Ring* poem, together with a preface outlining his plan for a special *Ring* festival. Only a rich monarch could sponsor such a project: 'Will such a prince appear?' he had asked. When Ludwig read those words he knew that *he* was the prince. Since he was twelve or thirteen he had loved Wagner, shared his ideals, read all his prose works, memorized the words of his operas and thrilled to specially commanded performances. As a boy, he loved his father's country castle where large paintings of German legends covered the walls. The pictures of *Lohengrin* enthralled him most of all: in his romantic imagination he fancied himself as the Knight of the Swan and even had a Lohengrin-armour made which he wore sometimes when he was king. The reign ahead of him was full of sorrow, but neither he nor Wagner feared future tragedy at their rapturous first meeting in 1864. They had so much to talk about and plan. Never again need Wagner earn a living by conducting concerts or sacrificing his works to inferior commercial theatres. The choice performances of his dreams would be given in Munich and transform existing standards of production in Germany. The King would give him 4,000 florins a year—more than the earnings of a judge or cabinet minister—plus a rent-free house where he could fulfil his great projects in peace. A huge lump sum of 16,500 florins would compensate for loss of other earnings while he wrote

The Ring for Ludwig, and additional money gifts would sort out his Vienna debts. He was not only solvent now, but rich! He wrote to his old friends and urged them to come and share his charmed existence: he would need their help in founding the new opera-house and music school he and the King were planning. Cornelius and Bülow arrived by the end of the year and were found royal appointments. Cosima appointed herself the guardian of his well-being and rarely left his side.

A letter from Wagner to King Ludwig

The coming of these and his other satellites caused murmurings among the musicians of Munich who felt themselves threatened by the newcomers. The political leaders were uneasy too. They feared the influence of this free-thinking, disreputable ex-revolutionary on their impressionable young King, and were quite horrified to discover Ludwig's plan to build a lavish new theatre just for him. They tried to discredit him in royal eyes through a smear campaign in the press, but Ludwig took no notice. 'Would that I could protect you against the lies of slanderers!' he wrote sadly to Wagner.

'Some day, dear one, it will be seen by everyone that the bond between us is pure, holy and eternal. . . . Some day their astonished eyes will behold the wonders that you and I together have dedicated to a better age than this. And so, have courage!'

Their first wonder was the production of *Tristan and Isolde*. At last Wagner had found the right singers for the title roles: Ludwig Schnorr von Carolsfeld and his wife Malvina from the Dresden Opera. Rehearsals began in the Munich Court Theatre on 10th April 1865, the very day on which Cosima gave birth to Wagner's daughter. She was called Isolde, naturally. It was an ecstatic time for Wagner. At last he was hearing his greatest music just as he had conceived it. Schnorr responded devotedly to his coaching and gave a breathtaking performance as Tristan. Nobody noticed how rotund he was when they heard him sing. The first performance took place in June, with Bülow conducting, and three more select performances followed. By the third, Schnorr was complaining of the icy draughts that chilled him from the wings while he was at the height of his passionate outpourings in Act Three. In mid-July he returned to Dresden, and on the 21st he was dead. 'Console my Richard,' were his last words. Wagner was crushed by the blow. He had lost his Siegfried-to-be, his truest interpreter and the model on whom young singers were to have been moulded in readiness for *The Ring*.

His hopes of a bright future in Munich gradually dimmed. The Cabinet created deliberate obstacles for the projected opera-house and music school and began to regard Wagner as a severe drain on the treasury. He was living in unbelievable luxury in his opulent new house and in his usual way was running up bills on all sides. He needed more money. In August he asked the King to double his annual salary and to give him at once the staggering sum of 40,000 florins. Ministerial hackles bristled. Why *should* the taxpayers of Bavaria support this preposterous foreigner and his sybaritic tastes? They almost persuaded Ludwig against granting so huge a sum—but Wagner's wishes prevailed. Cosima went to the treasury to collect the money and had to hire two coaches to carry all the bags of coin home.

It was this victory that caused Wagner's downfall. His power over Ludwig had proved stronger than that of the ministers, so now they would have to destroy him. Articles in the Munich papers attacked him savagely, and goaded him into an angry retort declaring that Bavaria would be a better place for the removal of certain of the King's ministers. Now he could be seen to be interfering with politics, the indignant Cabinet demanded his banishment. Church leaders, nobles and councillors united in presenting petitions, appeals and deputations to the King: Wagner must go. And so it was. Ludwig bowed to the inevitable and in December banished Wagner—for six months at least. After that time had elapsed he felt sure it would be safe to recall his hero, but Wagner knew he would not be returning. He went to Switzerland and resumed work on *The Mastersingers*. Cosima came to him in March and together they went hunting for the home of their dreams. They discovered an enchanting white house called 'Triebschen', overlooking Lake Lucerne: Ludwig sent money to pay the rent and Wagner moved in. For the next year or two, Cosima and the children divided their time between Lucerne and Munich. Bülow had always regarded his brilliant wife as a superior being and knew now that she was Wagner's true complement. He had devoted his life to Wagner's cause, and even after his wife was taken from him, stifled his pain and continued his mission at a distance. Wagner, Napoleon and Bismarck, he said, were the three great spirits of the nineteenth century and as such were above the petty moralities of normal people.

Normal people, however, had normal thoughts about Wagner and his triangle. In the Munich press the anti-Wagner campaign thrived on gossipy insinuations about the separate comings and goings of Frau and Herr von Bülow. It was vital to all three parties that the King should not lose faith in them: Wagner needed royal money, Cosima her good name, and Hans the directorship of the new music school. The royal idealist had no doubts as to the unblemished honour of his friends, and signed a public declaration saying so. Perhaps Wagner felt a little shame at the deception? Poor Ludwig was desperately unhappy without him. On the composer's fifty-third birthday he stole away from Munich and came to 'Triebschen'. He wanted to abdicate so he could be for ever at Wagner's side, but was reminded that only as King could he put their cherished plans into action. The staging of *The Mastersingers* was their next objective. By the end of September, Act Two was finished, and over the winter, Act Three.

In February 1867 his second daughter, Eva, was born at 'Triebschen'. Never before had such peace and joy surrounded his domestic life. A young visitor staying at the house was privileged to share its tranquil atmosphere: he was Hans Richter, one day to be a great Wagnerian conductor, but for the present the master's copyist. He was most impressed by the style of the household, with its staff of housekeeper, housemaid, governess, nursemaid, cook, valet and bootboy, and its menagerie of two peacocks, two dogs, two cats and one horse. It was hardly surprising that Wagner refused Ludwig's requests to leave his country haven and return to Munich. He did spend a few weeks at Hans's and Cosima's house there in summer, supervising performances of *Tannhäuser* and *Lohengrin* commanded by the King. The *Lohengrin* turned out to be less than ideal. Wagner invited Tichatschek, now aged sixty, to sing the title role, and at the dress rehearsal Ludwig was so upset to see an aged face and body masquerading as the young hero of his dreams that he ordered a different Lohengrin to be found before the performance. The rift was soon healed, and in the autumn Ludwig and Wagner launched the new music school, and a journal propagating the gospel of German regeneration through the music-drama.

Early the next year rehearsals for *The Mastersingers* began, with Bülow directing the orchestra and Richter the chorus. On 21st June a distinguished audience from all over Europe gathered to witness the first performance. The Overture told them a good deal about what lay in store, for like that for *Tannhäuser* it summarizes the philosophical content of the drama. In this case it is not good and evil that vie with one another, but the old and the

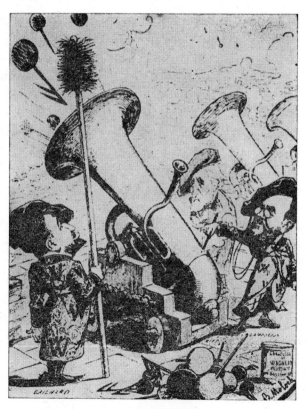

The 'Wagner tuba'

new, the strict and the free. The Mastersingers are an ancient guild of musicians who have gained the rank of 'Master' by composing songs in accordance with certain cast-iron rules. The young knight Walther is auditioned by the guild, but shocks them with a very different sort of song, one inspired only by the feelings of his heart. In the end neither side wins outright: instead, the traditional rules of the Mastersingers are combined with Walther's more live and spontaneous art to create still greater music for Germany. The Overture begins with two themes describing the guild. The first is rather pompous and pedantic, but noble, like the worthy Mastersingers themselves. The second is a march, proud and glorious like the great heritage the guild so strictly upholds. Both are richly scored for a large orchestra with plenty of brass instruments: he always liked to have a good number of these to add weight and grandeur to the tone. He even invented a new brass instrument, the 'Wagner tuba', used in *The Ring* to fill the gap between horn and trombone sound.

The Mastersingers: two extracts from the Overture

Liszt with his daughter, Cosima

Richard Wagner, *c.* 1865

Wagner and his wife, Cosima

The Wagners' house at Bayreuth, the Villa
Wahnfried

The Palazzo-Calergi on the Grand Canal, Venice, where Wagner died in 1883

Wagner's grave at the Villa Wahnfried
shortly before it was closed

A pencil sketch of Wagner the evening
before he died, drawn by Paul von
Joukowsky in Cosima's diary

King Ludwig to the Rescue

On the first night Ludwig made Wagner sit with him in the royal box—a scandalous infraction of etiquette—and from there he acknowledged the tumultuous applause at the end of the evening. The mud-slingers of Munich could not tolerate his success and filled the papers with new slanders. Wagner felt ill and tired and vowed he would never go back there again. Once that decision was made there was no longer any need for the triangle to present a respectable front to authority. In November 1868 Cosima went to him at 'Triebschen', and this time stayed for good.

X

The Ring is Rounded

At last it was time to wake up Siegfried and continue his adventures from the point they had reached eleven years ago. As the third of the great *Ring* dramas reached completion in June 1869, Cosima presented him with a Siegfried of his own, the son he had always longed for.

A world away in Munich, Ludwig had commanded the first performance of *The Rhinegold*. It presented many novel problems of stagecraft, like the underwater swimming of the Rhinemaidens, and Wagner knew full well that it might all fail without his surveillance—but he had made up his mind to have no more dealings with Munich or the Court Theatre, the manager of which he vigorously detested. He wrote strong letters to the King, telling him to dismiss the manager or else withdraw the production. Ludwig took no notice and the rehearsals went ahead. At the eleventh hour Richter, the conductor, flatly refused to direct with such awful scenery: Wagner had instructed him to make this gesture. The King *ordered* him to conduct, and he declined, saying he would only obey Wagner's wishes. Ludwig was furious and contemplated cutting off Wagner's salary. He sacked Richter, engaged a local conductor and had his performances of *The Rhinegold* in September. When he had had his way he healed the breach with the composer, but not before Wagner had made him truly contrite for wilfully staging his work like an ordinary opera, with journalists and the paying public for an audience and not the choice array of kindred spirits they had envisaged. The unfortunate Ludwig could scarcely be blamed for wanting to see the existing portions of *The Ring* under *any* conditions since he had paid handsomely enough for them and was their rightful owner.

In the haven of 'Triebschen' all was peace. Cosima worshipped him and was completely absorbed in tending his every need. He dictated to her the autobiography which the King had requested. Together they read their

78

favourite books, played piano duets, enjoyed their children and wished only that Liszt could forgive them their indiscretions. His work flourished: the latter part of *The Ring* progressed, and numerous essays were added to his list of prose works. 'Reminiscences of Rossini' (whom he had met briefly in Paris), 'Recollections of Ludwig Schnorr', 'On Conducting' and 'Beethoven' were some of them. He basked in plentiful adulation from the fanatics who came from far and near to visit him. Two of his favourites were Judith Gautier, beautiful daughter of the French poet, and the philosopher Nietzsche, at the age of twenty-four a professor at nearby Basle University. For the time being, the young genius shared Wagner's views on Greek drama and his love of Schopenhauer; only later, after he had written books in praise of Wagnerian theories did his ideas change and his adulation turn to hatred.

One evening in March 1870 Wagner and Cosima read in an encyclopedia that the little Bavarian town of Bayreuth possessed the theatre with the largest stage in all Germany. The idea of presenting *The Ring* there struck him at once, though he breathed not a word about it to Ludwig. The unhappy King was having a harrowing time, for Germany and France were drifting implacably towards war. He needed the balm of Wagner's music even more than usual and was determined to hear *The Valkyrie* in Munich however much its composer may rage and fret. And so the second *Ring* opera was produced in the summer. Nothing could spoil Wagner's personal happiness just then because Cosima's divorce had come through and in August they were married at last. The deep devotion he felt for her and their baby son has been immortalized in some exquisite music he surprised her with the next Christmas Day—her birthday. Richter had secretly rehearsed a small orchestra, well out of earshot, and learned his own thirteen-bar trumpet part; he had to row out to the middle of the lake to do his practice as there was no hope of concealing trumpet noises in the house! On Christmas morning the players stood on the stairs outside Cosima's bedroom and Wagner conducted the first performance of the *Siegfried Idyll*. Appropriately enough, the themes were mostly drawn from the love music of Siegfried and Brünnhilde in the closing scene of *Siegfried*. Wagner wove these melodies together most lovingly to create a piece full of lullaby tenderness. The extract given here has been arranged for violin and piano.

The opening from *Siegfried Idyll*

F

When spring came they went to Bayreuth. A quick inspection of the historic theatre showed that it would not do at all for their plans since the auditorium, unlike the stage, was minute. 'So we shall have to build,' Cosima wrote in her diary. Bayreuth seemed ideal for Wagner's festival, a quiet, unspoilt country town where no rival attractions existed to detract from the performances; a place where people could relax quietly during the day and prepare themselves for the spiritual feast to come at dusk; a town moreover situated in his protector's kingdom. He went straight to the delighted municipal authorities and began to negotiate a building site. No sooner were his intentions made public than other towns jealously vied with Bayreuth to offer bigger and better locations; even London and Chicago made him offers, but his heart was already committed. In no time at all he was in the thick of fund-raising activities: in Berlin, Leipzig and all the big German cities, 'Wagner societies' were founded to sponsor concerts and whip up a fever of enthusiasm. Those people who donated to the building fund would be invited to the festival: there was to be no ticket-selling of the ordinary sort.

The design of the theatre was closely supervised by Wagner along the lines of the projected Munich building. Simplicity was to be its keynote. No fussy ornamentation would distract attention from the stage, and each and every seat would have a clear and uninterrupted view. There would not even be the up-and-down of baton and violin bows to catch the eye since the whole orchestra was to be housed under the stage and hooded off from public view. The building would be made of cheap materials as a temporary structure to be pulled down in favour of something more substantial once the festival was gloriously established: in fact it stands to this day in its original state, its perfect acoustics preserved intact. Ludwig was very gracious about giving up his right to produce the rest of *The Ring* in Munich and gave Wagner the money to build himself a grand house in Bayreuth. Soon after the last act sketch of *Götterdämmerung* was concluded, excavations for the theatre began.

Now the divine days at 'Triebschen' were ended, and Wagner and Cosima, with their extensive household of children and servants and musical assistants, moved into a hotel in Bayreuth. A month later, on his fifty-ninth birthday, he laid the foundation stone before great crowds of well-wishers. 'Be blessed, my stone, stand long and hold firm!' he said, as he hammered it into place. Afterwards there was a lot of speech-making and then a sublime performance of Beethoven's Ninth Symphony, conducted by Wagner in the old theatre. Since 1951 this work so dear to his heart has been played

F*

annually at the festival, making a solitary exception to the all-Wagner programme structure.

When the festivities were over he quietly went back to work on the last monumental instalment of *The Ring*. But the Bayreuth enterprise would give him little peace and he often had to lay down his pen and deal with the business complications that cropped up. He had to spend time seeking out the right singers too, and had scarcely returned from a talent-scouting tour of the opera-houses late in 1872 before he was obliged to set out again and conduct concerts to bolster up the theatre fund. Despite the best efforts of the Wagner societies, the required patrons were woefully tardy in making

Wagner the supreme

their donations and by midsummer 1873 it was obvious that the existing cash supplies would only offset the cost of the four bare walls. Unless a large lump sum was found quickly, the building would have to stop. In October an anxious meeting of the Wagner societies assembled in Bayreuth to discuss the situation. They launched appeals in all directions: to the theatres to give benefit performances; to book- and music-sellers to display subscription forms, and to the German people in general. But in the end it was none of these who guaranteed Bayreuth's survival, but the ever-faithful Ludwig.

For all his sadness that Wagner had deserted him and the Munich theatre so gladly placed at his disposal, the King could not let his idol down now, though he hardened himself against his appeals for some months. In the end, 'it would be lunacy to believe in any decline of my ardour for you and your great undertaking,' he wrote. 'No, No and again No! It shall not end thus! Help must be given! Our plan must not fail!' And so the building went on, and the festival opening was fixed for 1876.

XI

Bayreuth Established

Never had Bayreuth experienced such ferocious activity as shook it the next two years. Wagner was like a man possessed, organizing every last detail with driving, superhuman energy. Had he been less arrogant, less convinced of his exalted mission to art, more merely human, there would have been no festival. The obstacles he overcame were staggering—and not the least of them was persuading the cream of German artists to give him weeks of their services free of charge. 'Whoever will not come to me for the honour and out of enthusiasm can stay where he is,' he stated. 'I do not give a jot for a singer who will only come to me for one of those fantastic fees. A creature like that could never live up to my artistic requirements.' Famous singers accepted with alacrity the summons to Bayreuth, and most of them submitted humbly to the stripping down of their performing technique and its reconstruction on Wagnerian lines.

The preliminary rehearsals took place around the piano at 'Wahnfried', Wagner's imposing new home. Casting dilemmas still gave him many a sleepless night for a Siegfried was yet to be found. Eventually a young tenor called George Unger, with an enormous frame and a faulty voice, was discovered. Wagner persuaded him to tear up his Mannheim contract and spend a full year at Bayreuth, learning singing with a specially imported teacher and acting with Wagner himself. Even his outlook on life was reshaped by the master till it bore closer resemblance to Siegfried's dauntless optimism.

Before the major rehearsals of 1875 Wagner had to go out and earn some money to pay the fares and living expenses of his artists, who would soon descend on Bayreuth from all over Germany. The theatre was swallowing up every coin that had been donated, and quickly devoured the receipts of this latest concert tour as well. He conducted in Budapest, Berlin, and in Vienna where Liszt, now reconciled to his 'terrible fille' and her husband, added lustre to the programme by playing Beethoven's *Emperor Concerto*.

86

At the rehearsals he told the players how to play and the singers how to sing, and showed them how to act by his brilliant miming. When they had all gone back to their own opera-houses he went tirelessly on, raising money for the furnishings, the sets, the lighting, the complex stage machinery. He supervised *Lohengrin* and *Tannhäuser* in Vienna—and met the fifteen-year-old Hugo Wolf. He directed *Tristan* in Berlin. He wrote a march for the centenary of the American Declaration of Independence—and freely admitted that the best thing about it was the 5,000 dollar cheque he received for it. Against all odds he made the theatre ready in time for the festival to begin.

Three complete cycles of *The Ring* were given, plus a private one for Ludwig who hated being gaped at by crowds. He arrived by private train at dead of night and was met by Wagner at a deserted railway halt outside the town. The disappointed townsfolk caught only glimpses of his closed carriage as it sped to and from the theatre, but he at least was happy: his years of longing for *The Ring* were over. How he must have thrilled to the great exploits of Siegfried, and to the heroic music that characterizes him so strongly. The joyous call of his horn ringing through the forest is the perfect reflection of his fearless and optimistic nature. Here it is, in the version that opens 'Siegfried's Rhine Journey' from Act Three of *Götterdämmerung*. It leads into the Rhine motive, three forms of which appear on p. 51.

From Act III of *Götterdämmerung*

Ludwig loved it all so much that he suffered the company of other crowned heads and came again to the third cycle. Never had such a dazzling array of royalty gathered together to grace a musical event. The Emperor of Brazil was there, and the German Kaiser, and quantities of princes, grand-dukes and lordlings. Wagner was the most eulogized composer alive, a legend in his own lifetime, a unique figure in musical history. With incredible tenacity he had transformed a wild dream into tangible reality, and every imaginable celebrity was there to honour him.

But when it was all over and Valhalla had gone up in flames for the last time, he was tired to the very core. His herculean labours had taken years off his life, and he knew it. He took his family to Italy and spent the autumn there recovering his strength and brooding over the enormous outstanding debts. He had hoped to present an even better festival the following year, but there was no chance of that until the theatre was solvent. Instead he spent the next summer in London, conducting concerts at the Albert Hall, a venture which reduced the debt by a mere £700. Not surprisingly, he was bitter; with his own sweat and tears he had erected a temple to German art and now the worshippers refused to pay. He thought of throwing up everything and settling in America—but that was more than one votary could bear. Ludwig knew he would have to help out although he had almost bankrupted Bavaria with his own crazy architectural schemes. (After the intrigues that tore him apart from Wagner he had turned bitterly away from public life and resorted to building fantastic castles with a strongly Wagnerian air about them. One featured a Venus grotto, a Hunding's hut and a Good Friday meadow. Another, the most incredible of all, Neuschwanstein, is a fairy-tale knights' castle in medieval style, where Tannhäuser and Lohengrin would have felt quite at home. Its glistening white towers surmount a high mountain peak, up and down which the builders had to climb for seventeen years. Even the kitchen taps are in the shape of swans' heads.) He drew up a document decreeing that the takings from all Wagner productions in Munich should be devoted to liquidating the debt; thus a great weight was lifted from the composer's ageing shoulders.

Wagner worked off his anger against the Germany that had disappointed him in numerous scathing articles in the *Bayreuther Blätter*, a journal he founded himself. His pontifications on all sorts of other subjects appeared there too, including pronouncements against vivisection and for vegetarianism. He kept up a regular correspondence with Judith Gautier, and commissioned her to send all manner of exotic perfumeries to him from Paris. With their sweet odours drifting about him he composed his last work: *Parsifal*. The legend of the Holy Grail from which Christ drank at the Last Supper had impressed him long ago, in the far-off summer days at Marienbad where *Lohengrin* and *The Mastersingers* had their genesis. Like several of his works, it rested within him for many years before the right time came for its composition. Now he was an old man. He had preached fiery reforms to the world and they had gone unheeded; he had held out in *The Ring* a terrible vision of cosmic destruction—and now he took pity on himself and sick humanity and turned to the one last hope, the redemption of mankind through Divine Love. For this final work he had reserved his most beautiful musical description of nature. The great forests and rivers and landscapes of the Rhineland had always been there in his music, but here he turns with reverence to a very special scene. It is the transfigured meadow at which Parsifal gazes spellbound on Good Friday. On that day, according to legend, all nature smiles with joy in gratitude for Christ's sacrifice, and every flower of the field radiates a heavenly light.

'Good Friday Music' from *Parsifal*

From 1877 to 1882 he worked at the score, sometimes at 'Wahnfried', sometimes in Italy (his frequent refuge from the ruinous Bayreuth weather). Progress was slow because of his failing health and the hours he devoted to his adoring visitors. On his way back to Bayreuth at the end of 1880 he visited the King in Munich for the last time. As the Prelude to *Parsifal* was complete he was able to conduct a private hearing of it, but managed to take offence when the royal auditor greedily demanded a repetition, and *then* the *Lohengrin* Prelude to follow.

The year 1882 saw the production of *Parsifal* at Bayreuth. Since he no longer had any illusions about the efficiency of Wagner societies and donation schemes, the sixteen superlative performances were attended by the paying public. On the last night when he noticed that Hermann Levi, the conductor, seemed unwell, he discreetly took the baton from him during the last act. It was the one and only time he conducted publicly in his own theatre. His sacred music-drama made a profound impression; though the unctuous shook their heads over the enactment of the Communion service on stage, the faithful accepted the divine music, and subject, in the spirit of its creator.

His work was over now and his heart was weakening. *The Ring* was making its way throughout Europe, and he was glad of it. He spent his last months at a palace in Venice with his family, and delighted Cosima with a birthday-present performance of his youthful *Symphony in C*. He planned another *Parsifal* festival for the next summer and drafted a few ideas for articles. On 13th February 1883 he died in Cosima's arms after a heart attack.

By gondola and train his body was carried home to Bayreuth. At the station a band played Siegfried's Funeral March, and a choir sang the chorus he had written for Weber's posthumous home-coming. Black flags fluttered from every house as the procession made its way through packed streets to 'Wahnfried'. There, in his own grounds, was laid to rest one of the greatest musicians and most controversial men the world has known. As for Ludwig, in 1886 he was declared insane, and a few days after was found drowned with his keeper in Lake Starnberg. He had always said he could not bear to live once Wagner was dead.

XII

The Aftermath

Cosima cared for the festival as she had done for Wagner, and added model productions of all his operas from *The Flying Dutchman* onwards to the Bayreuth repertoire. She died, a very old lady, in 1930, but had long since handed over the theatre to the care of Siegfried. When he died, his wife, and then his sons took over. Now one of them, Wieland, outstanding among modern producers, is dead, and his brother Wolfgang directs the festival alone. In the early days it took place mostly every other year but at Hitler's wish became an annual event. Every summer devotees from all over the world make the pilgrimage to Bayreuth and find both town and festival much as Wagner left them.

As he wished, the performances begin at four o'clock in the afternoon and spread themselves over the rest of the day. During the hour-long intervals between acts, people stroll on the terraces or relax in the peaceful wooded gardens until a resounding brass fanfare summons them back for the next episode in the saga. He would be pleased to know that his grandsons' productions are as influential as were his own, though vastly different in style. Today his explicit instructions about the appearance of dragons, bears, rams and the like are disregarded (which he probably would not have minded since he was never very happy with the way stage machinists realized such requirements). The symbolic productions of today put the music to the fore—and keep the name of Wagner as contentious as ever it was.

No other opera composer has exerted such influence as he on the subsequent development of music. Bruckner, Mahler, Wolf, Richard Strauss, Humperdinck, Schoenberg, Duparc, Chausson, Debussy—the names of those who fell under his spell are endless. Some benefited from the enchantment; others in fighting it off discovered whole new musical horizons. For some time after his death many opera composers were obsessed with creating their own mythological music-dramas. Several appeared in Germany and

France; and in England, Rutland Boughton dreamed of founding a festival theatre to stage his sagas of King Arthur. But no imitation could approach the originals in stature, for the monumental epics created by Wagner are the measure of the man himself, and such giants are born but rarely.

Suggestions for Further Reading

Since Wagner is the most written-about of all composers there is plenty to choose from. His autobiography *My Life* tells his story up to 1864 when King Ludwig rescued him. An interesting selection of his correspondence with various people is contained in *Letters of Richard Wagner: the Burrell Collection* (Gollancz). Ernest Newman's *The Life of Richard Wagner* (Knopf, 4 vols.) is probably the best biography of a composer ever written and gives the fullest possible account of his life. The same author's *Wagner Operas* (Knopf) describes the plot and music of each music-drama in great detail. The history of the Bayreuth Festival from Wagner's day to this is told by Geoffrey Skelton in *Wagner at Bayreuth* (Braziller). A book with many fascinating pictures relating to the composer is *Wagner; a pictorial biography* by Walter Panofsky (Thames and Hudson). *Wagner's Ring and its Symbols* by Robert Donington (St. Martin's, paperback) gives some of the many symbolic interpretations that can be read into the *Ring*. The second half of *Wagner* by Robert L. Jacobs (Farrar, Straus and Giroux) examines the musical content of all the main works.

Short Summary of Wagner's Works

Operas and Music-Dramas

Die Feen (The Fairies), 1833–4
Das Liebesverbot (The Love Ban), 1835–6
Rienzi, 1838–40
Der Fliegende Holländer (The Flying Dutchman), 1841
Tannhäuser, 1843–4
Lohengrin, 1846–8
Der Ring des Nibelungen (The Ring of the Nibelungs), 1853–74
   Das Rheingold (The Rhine Gold), 1853–4
   Die Walküre (The Valkyrie), 1854–6
   Siegfried, 1856–69
   Götterdämmerung (Twilight of the Gods), 1869–74
Tristan und Isolde, 1857–9
Die Meistersinger von Nürnberg (The Mastersingers of Nuremberg), 1862–7
Parsifal

Orchestral Works

Symphony in C major, 1832
A Faust Overture, 1840
Siegfried Idyll, 1870
Overtures and Marches

Choral Works

Neujahrs Kantate (New Year Cantata), for chorus and orchestra, 1834
Das Liebesmahl der Apostel (The Love Feast of the Apostles), for men's chorus and orchestra, 1843
An Webers Grab (At Weber's Grave), for unaccompanied men's chorus, 1844
Patriotic choruses

Short Summary of Wagner's Works

Piano Works

Polonaise in D for four hands, 1831
Album Sonata in E flat, 1853
Album pieces

Songs

Five Poems of Mathilde Wesendonck, 1857–8
Songs in German and French

Literary Works

Collected in twelve volumes. There is an eight-volume English version, translated by W. Ashton Ellis

Index